SpringerBriefs in Business

For further volumes:
http://www.springer.com/series/8860

Ibrahim Sirkeci

Transnational Marketing and Transnational Consumers

Springer

Ibrahim Sirkeci
Faculty of Business and Management
Regent's Centre for Transnational Studies
Regent's University London
London, UK

ISSN 2191-5482 ISSN 2191-5490 (electronic)
ISBN 978-3-642-36774-8 ISBN 978-3-642-36775-5 (eBook)
DOI 10.1007/978-3-642-36775-5
Springer Heidelberg New York Dordrecht London

Library of Congress Control Number: 2013938742

© The Author(s) 2013
This work is subject to copyright. All rights are reserved by the Publisher, whether the whole or part of the material is concerned, specifically the rights of translation, reprinting, reuse of illustrations, recitation, broadcasting, reproduction on microfilms or in any other physical way, and transmission or information storage and retrieval, electronic adaptation, computer software, or by similar or dissimilar methodology now known or hereafter developed. Exempted from this legal reservation are brief excerpts in connection with reviews or scholarly analysis or material supplied specifically for the purpose of being entered and executed on a computer system, for exclusive use by the purchaser of the work. Duplication of this publication or parts thereof is permitted only under the provisions of the Copyright Law of the Publisher's location, in its current version, and permission for use must always be obtained from Springer. Permissions for use may be obtained through RightsLink at the Copyright Clearance Center. Violations are liable to prosecution under the respective Copyright Law. The use of general descriptive names, registered names, trademarks, service marks, etc. in this publication does not imply, even in the absence of a specific statement, that such names are exempt from the relevant protective laws and regulations and therefore free for general use.
While the advice and information in this book are believed to be true and accurate at the date of publication, neither the authors nor the editors nor the publisher can accept any legal responsibility for any errors or omissions that may be made. The publisher makes no warranty, express or implied, with respect to the material contained herein.

Printed on acid-free paper

Springer is part of Springer Science+Business Media (www.springer.com)

Dedicated to Dr. Joanne Stansfield

Preface

The ways in which mobility and movement play a role in marketing and international business and management are of interest in an increasingly fast moving and interconnected world. An ever growing number of people are pursuing transnational lives along with increasing connectivity beyond national borders. Similarly, more and more firms are doing business crossing and beyond national borders. Hence, *Transnational Marketing* and *Transnational Consumers* are becoming increasingly common in today's globalising and fast-moving world of business. This book is offering a fresh perspective focusing on the transnational character of organisations and firms, while underlining the importance of the transnationality of marketing strategies for success. At the same time, it introduces the novel concept of 'transnational consumers' and 'transnational mobile consumers' which takes into account the increasing human mobility and its implications for marketing success. This book gives flesh to the ever popular shorthand "glocal" referring to strategies thinking globally but acting locally. This is the reality of current business environment where the norm is fast mobility of goods, services, finance and consumers.

Wider marketing literature has so far simply name dropped but never attempted to define what "transnational marketing" is. Thus, this business brief is a pioneering attempt in clarifying the concepts and understanding this increasingly important phenomenon. The book offers clear and crisp definitions of what is global, international, multinational and transnational. It defines *Transnational Marketing* as *understanding and addressing customer needs, wants and desires in their own country of residence and beyond and in borderless cultural contexts with the help of synergies emerging across national boundaries and transfer of expertise and advantages between markets where the organization operates transnationally with a transnational mentality supported by transnational organization structures and without compromising the sustainability of any target markets and resource environment offering satisfactory exchanges between the parties involved.* It explains with examples and illustrations the key features of a transnational marketing strategy which is a recipe for success for today's global organisations, large and small alike.

vii

Key terminology are also highlighted and summarised in a glossary. In this book, mobility and movement are introduced into marketing thinking in an ever more mobile world. A truly business brief which offers cutting edge thinking in a concise fashion.

I would like to thank many people who made this book possible and inspired and supported me throughout. It includes tens of postgraduate students I did teach at European Business School, Regent's University London and particularly Martina Drennow, Evinc Dogan and Prashanth Mahagaonkar, as well as Nikolaus Curtius, Ivelina Georgieva, Cagri Haksoz, Svend Hollensen, Veerapa Jiravong, Monika Koller, Krzyztof Kubacki, Richard Mannix, Simon O'Leary, Maktoba Omar, Assia Rolls and Ebru Sucak. I also thank the editors and production team at Springer.

London, UK   Ibrahim Sirkeci

Contents

1 Transnationalisation and Transnational Marketing Strategy 1
  1.1   Introduction 1
  1.2   Transnationalisation in a Global Era 4
  1.3   Transnationality of Organisations 5
  1.4   Transnational Marketing and Transnational
       Marketing Strategy 12
  References 21

**2 Transnationals: Transnational Consumers and Transnational
Mobile Consumers** 25
  2.1   Connectedness and the Consumer E-Geography 27
  2.2   Introducing Mobility and Movement
       as Segmentation Variables 29
  2.3   Early Scholarship on Mobiles 30
  References 33

3 Mobility and the Transnationals 35
  3.1   Mobile Population is Larger Than Migrant Population 37
  3.2   Sub-groups Within Transnational Mobiles 39
       3.2.1   Transnational Professionals and High
             Skilled Migrants 40
       3.2.2   Transnational Entrepreneurs 43
       3.2.3   Wealthy Mobiles 44
       3.2.4   Tourists and Visitors 45
       3.2.5   Students 46
       3.2.6   Immigrants 46
  3.3   Segmentation for Transnationals and Mobiles 51
  References 54

**4 Targeting and Reaching Transnationals
and Transnational Mobiles** 59
  References 62

5 Conclusions 65
    References 67

About the Author 69

Index 71

Abbreviations

EPRG	Ethnocentric, Polycentric, Regiocentric, Geocentric
EU	European Union
Fb	Facebook
FDI	Foreign Direct Investment
GDP	Gross Domestic Product
H&M	Hennes and Mauritz
MNC	Multinational Corporation
MEP	Member of European Parliament
MNE	Multinational Enterprise
NAFTA	North American Free Trade Agreement
NGO	Non-governmental Organisation
OECD	Organisation for Economic Co-operation and Development
SBU	Strategic Business Unit
TNC	Transnational Corporation
TNI	Transnationality Index
UN	United Nations
UNCTAD	United Nations Conference on Trade and Development
UNHCR	United Nations High Commissioner for Refugees
UNICEF	United Nations Children's Fund
WHM	Working Holiday Maker
WIPS	World Investment Prospects Survey

Chapter 1
Transnationalisation and Transnational Marketing Strategy

1.1 Introduction

Bartlett, Ghoshal, and Stonehouse are among the very few scholars who argued over the years that transnational strategy is either superior to other strategies or it is the ultimate level to reach for success. This is pretty much all one would find in a very few textbooks on international management. However, these accounts of transnational marketing remains rather abstract and unsubstantiated while also lacking theoretical depth. Perhaps the theoretical depth issue is common to all management sub-disciplines. For example, Burton claimed that weakness of marketing scholarship and theory is due to "a lack of theorists, lack of theory courses, business school strategies and misguided perceptions of practitioner-oriented research amongst other things" (Burton 2005). Nevertheless, here we are trying to add another brick to marketing and management theory.

The world is in a constant change as are the organisations, the consumers and the ways in which businesses are connected and managed. The two main drastic changes we are concerned with here are, first, the increasing mobility of goods, finances and people and second, the enormous speed and variety available in communication and transportation. This has resulted in a rapid globalisation. Along with socio-economic growth registered in countries outside Western Europe and North America, such as in China, Brazil, India, Russia, Turkey, South Africa, Mexico and several others, we have witnessed relative improvements in living conditions and prosperity across the world. Many organisations have set up aggressive global strategies looking for wider coverage in world markets whilst also relocating certain functions to countries where cost and logistic advantages exist. Today's firms and organisations are increasingly involved in transnational businesses as such. The spread of global communication channels and 'universalist' cultural influences helped catalyse this process to an extent. Hence standardised products and services became a priority. However soon it has become apparent that local, national and regional differences in tastes, legal political frameworks, customs, habits and behaviour were significant. Thus organisations, firms and practitioners faced new challenges which are yet to be fully addressed.

I. Sirkeci, *Transnational Marketing and Transnational Consumers*,
SpringerBriefs in Business, DOI: 10.1007/978-3-642-36775-5_1,
© The Author(s) 2013

According to a Deloitte survey (Deloitte 2012), a majority of managers agree that current issues revolve around globalisation and geographical markets and, even more importantly, see global human mobility as a cure to the strategic challenges while only a small percentage (between 12 and 28 %) utilise global mobility to address these challenges. However, mobility of staff generally is not aligned with strategic business objectives, where it can make a real impact. Hence, within a transnational organisational structure, the mobility of staff is crucial for development of synergies and to enhance the national responsiveness in international marketing strategies through first-hand knowledge and experience.

At one level, intuitively many organisations and some scholars realised these challenges and came up with a combo term: 'Glocal' which refers to the need for globalisation on the one hand and localisation, adaptation and customisation on the other. The term's initial use in English goes back to the 1980s (see Simon-Miller 1986). However, this idea is not yet mature enough to result in a scholarly model in management and marketing.

Outside business and management, in other disciplines, transnationalism as an approach has been rather more developed. Therefore, we are indebted to those researchers and scholars in developing a transnational marketing concept and model. For example, indirectly related to business and management, in legal studies, the concept of transnational is not new. Hall and Biersteker uses the concept of "transnational private authority" referring to transnational religious movements, mafias and mercenaries (2002, p. 7). Apparently, such transnational authority is widely exercised by two types of coordination service firms; accounting firms and credit rating agencies[1] (Nolke and Perry 2007, p. 124).

It is also argued that transnationalism has been in existence in one way or another for over a century at least (Foner 1997). The key feature of the transnational perspective is the recognition of the interaction between the global and the local as well as the compromise due to the continuing power of nation states that moderates transnational movement of things, finances, ideas, and people. Transnational as an adjective was first used in 1921 and defined as "extending or going beyond national borders" according to *Webster's Dictionary* (1988, p. 1254).

In defining Transnationalism, Steven Vertovec states that it "broadly refers to multiple ties and interactions linking people or institutions across the borders of nation-states. Today myriad systems of relationship, exchange and mobility function intensively and in real time while being spread across the world. New technologies, especially involving telecommunications, serve to connect such networks. Despite great distances and notwithstanding the presence of international borders (and all the laws, regulations and national narratives they represent), many forms of association have been globally intensified and now take place paradoxically in a planet-spanning yet common arena of activity. In some instances transnational forms and processes serve to speed-up or exacerbate

---

[1] For example, two major agencies: Moody's Investor Service (Moody's) and Standard & Poor's (S&P).

historical patterns of activity, in others they represent arguably new forms of human interaction. Transnational practices and their consequent configurations of power are shaping the world of the twenty-first century." (Vertovec 2004, p. ii)[2]

He refers to the intensity and ever growing volume of real time businesses and exchanges enhanced and facilitated by mobility and new technologies creating world wide networks. Earlier, Basch et al. (1994, p. 6) define transnationalism as a "process by which immigrants forge and sustain multistranded social relations that link together their societies of origin and settlement" and they "call these processes transnationalism to emphasize that many immigrants today build social fields that cross geographic, cultural and political borders".

Transnationalism can be understood in a dialectic view of the links between 'the global' and 'the local' in a world of nodes denoting the *transnational space* where global and local are increasingly difficult to separate from each other (see Kearney 1995; Miller 1995, 1997; Grewal and Kaplan 1994; Jackson et al. 2004). Transnational marketing and management is about business and consumption practices in this very space. "Transnationality ... refers to a social space that transcends national boundaries; in this space, the 'national' is no longer the primary constitutive dimension of social relations, without however being relegated to complete irrelevance" (Vliegenhart and Overbeek 2007, p. 183). This transnational space is where economic and market exchanges take place. Therefore, it is the very place where a true transnational organization would stand and operate.

Transnational is an ironic term in a sense that it refers to the nation and yet it emphasises the blurring, transgressing, and breaking down the nations and national boundaries. Hence movements across nations and national boundaries become essential at the expense of the nation or national boundaries. The inspiration for this book came from studies on transnational migration, a field of study where the concept is allegedly most advanced. Transnational migrants are partly our focus here when it comes to transnational mobile consumers. One of the common references in these studies is to the transnational space and transnationality, which is not necessarily a physical space. We will come back to this non-physical nature of transnational space in later sections when transnational consumers are discussed.

This book provides insights and elaborates on two facets of the challenge: Considerations and ways in which organisations devise strategies suiting the needs of the firm and customers in an increasingly transnational world. The first aim of this book it to define what is a transnational marketing organisation, discussing the transnationality of organisations and the need to take into account the transnationality of marketing strategies. The second aim is to elaborate the concept of 'transnational consumers' and 'transnational mobile consumers' which is one of the drivers for the need for transnational marketing strategies and relates to a growing consumer segment across the world. First, the concept of transnationalism

---

[2] Vertovec in another paper argues "not all diasporas are transnational communities, but transnational communities arise within diasporas" (2005, p. 4). This is something one should challenge as in the era of *superfast* communication and transportation, individuals and groups including consumers may become transnational and show transnational behavior.

is introduced and linked to the management context by focusing on transnationality index (TNI), an instrument used for over two decades to measure the degree of transnationality of multinational firms. Following criticisms of this instrument (i.e. TNI), transnationality of marketing strategies will be discussed before moving onto the transnational consumers and the utility of mobility and movement in marketing segmentation. Hence, recent data and some case studies are used to illustrate existing practices and needs in developing transnational marketing and management strategies. The final section of the book ponders on managerial implications, limitations and potential future avenues in this line of scholarship.

1.2 Transnationalisation in a Global Era

Theodore Levitt, in his famous article, *Globalisation of Markets,* argued that there was a shift towards globalisation, i.e. standardised products was in place in response to convergence of demand across the globe (Levitt 1983). This has received criticism widely and rightly so (Tedlow and Abdelal 2004). Globalisation has perhaps passed its sell-by-date now and this is why scholars, researchers, managers and practitioners are seeking new vocabularies and approaches. When the term "glocal" introduced in a very catchy slogan "think global act local", many cheers were heard. However have we really grasped the meaning of it? What are the managerial and marketing implications of this "thinking global and acting local"? Perhaps more importantly, how can it be achieved?

Our students often ask what is the difference between global, international and multinational firms. Then they ask what makes the transnational distinct. In terms of production and marketing, multinationals offer products tailored for national markets, *the globals* offer standardized products for all markets, and internationals offer diversified products for a few or more markets. These terms also reflect their ownerships and organisational span across countries. The "transnational" firm emerges there as "stateless" or not belonging, or not affiliated, to any single nation. The answer goes along the lines that transnationals offer products which are optimised for global efficiency and yet customised, tailored to address local needs and desires in different markets by drawing resources from a variety of countries served.

One major drive for transnational marketing is the change in the marketing environment, which requires a transnational effort to achieve success. For example, Overbeek et al. (2007, pp. 207, 208) argue that transnational regulations increasingly replace domestic ones in Europe: Hence it means changing corporate governance procedures and regulations, and transnational private regulation replacing domestic accounting standards. For example, for marketing managers, this means the *transnationalisation* of the political-legal marketing environment.

A bigger question is about the uses and practicality of the 'nation' as a unit of analysis while there are strong commonalities across and beyond the boundaries of national economies, cultures, living spaces, tastes and practices. Factors explaining this variety, as well as commonalities, must surely be transnational in nature. Challenging the 'national approach' is important in terms of better understanding the environment and devising appropriate strategies to deal with the challenges and behaviour which transcend the artificial divide between the internal (domestic) and the external (international). For example, while there are transnational actors, such as the European Commission and the OECD Secretariat, there are also "transnationally mobile shareholders" and "transnationally mobile investors" (see Apeldoorn and Horn 2007, p. 83). However, "one societal force clearly appears to be at the centre of nearly all recent reforms of corporate governance regulations, that is, transnationally mobile capital, in particular global capital market actors." (Apeldoorn and Horn 2007, p. 213). The market place and organisations also face a challenge: Companies of all sizes have to engage in cross-border business for various reasons including saturated home markets, threat of competition from overseas, growing interdependence of world economics, and internationalisation of customers.

It is also important to note that such transnationality in the world of organisations and firms does not necessarily need to be dominated by private sector. Roger Altman, chair and CEO, Evercore Partners, and former U.S. deputy treasury secretary, is among those who see an inflection point: "Much of the world is turning a historic corner and heading into a period in which the role of the state will be larger and that of the private sector will be smaller" (Kimmitt et al. 2010, p. 57), since an increasing number of Transnational companies/corporations (TNCs) and cross-border investments are owned, supported, or favoured by governments (Kimmitt et al. 2010, p. 61).

1.3 Transnationality of Organisations

The number of firms organised and operating transnationally is increasing and thus making borders less of a barrier. One can speak of "borderless" or "stateless" firms. In the same vein, we can even call some firms "born transnational". The concepts of transnational and transnationalism are not alien to management and economics in general. The *Journal of Transnational Management* was launched in 1996 even though the definitions of transnational management and transnational marketing are not yet finalised. The United Nations Conference on Trade and Development (UNCTAD) has focused on TNCs since the mid-1960s and in their 1991 World Investment Report, TNCs were described as "integrating agents" (UNCTAD 1991, p. 81). Later, in 1993, UNCTAD developed its infamous transnationality index, and in 2007, addressing some of the criticisms, a transnationality spread index was included in their analyses (UNCTAD 2007, p. 2).

Hollensen states that "transnational organizations include international companies that attempt to coordinate and integrate operations across national boundaries so as to achieve potential synergies on a global scale. Common R&D and frequent geographical exchange of human resources across borders are among the characteristics of a transnational organization. The transnational organisation's overall goal would be achieving global competitiveness through recognizing cross-border market similarities and differences" (2007, p. 363). This needs to be considered in the light of business mentalities in internationalization. From a marketing environment point of view, legal and political frameworks are also of importance for transnationals. Wigger (2007, p. 110) argues that "Transnational companies (TNCs) are genuinely interested in lifting regulatory barriers that hamper the free flow of capital accumulation"[3] because "reviews of cross-border intercompany agreements involving several jurisdictions increase transaction costs and the probability of conflicting results". Hence lifting these barriers is imperative for organisations that are operating across and above national borders.

Hearn (2004) also summarised approaches to, and definitions of, transnational corporations. Accordingly, some take a limited perspective and argue that for a corporation to be called transnational, both management and ownership must be equally divided between the two or more nations (Parhizgar 1999). Alternatively, these corporations are to be actors transcending the nations and the larger ones are often economically bigger than some nations (Bauman 1995; Giddens 1997).

Harzing (2000, p. 101) criticised the lack of clarity in conceptualisation of multinational corporations (MNCs) in the international business literature: Terms such as polycentric, geocentric, ethnocentric, multi-domestic, global, and trans-national are often used to indicate different types of MNCs. However, few studies tested these typologies which have become standard text book material. Hence it is quite common that *Multinational* and *Transnational* are used interchangeably when referring to large corporations such as Unilever, BP, Glaxo-Smith and the likes. Global companies are often described as more efficient while multinationals are considered more responsive to local differences. International companies demonstrate neither of these advantages. *Transnationals* systematically combine the efficiencies as *globals* and responsiveness as *multinationals* in their organi-sation configurations and operations.

The only simply operationalized definition of transnational organisation comes from the United Nations. According to the 2010–2012 World Investment Survey (UN 2012) examining 236 TNCs report that about 80 % companies reported more than 50 % of their *sales* to be abroad, nearly 55 % reported more than 50 % of their *employment* to be abroad and more than 40 % expected to have majority of their *assets* and *investments* to be abroad (Table 1.1). Also over two thirds of these 236 surveyed TNCs described themselves as "global". The United Nations Conference on Trade and Development World Investment Report 2011 (UNCTAD 2011) states that there are about 65,000 TNCs worldwide, 650 of which are state-owned.[4] Accordingly, about a quarter of global gross domestic product (GDP) is

---

[3] Often referred to in "Eurojargon" euphemistically as 'creating a level playing field' (Wigger 2007, p. 110).

[4] "State-owned TNC" is contradicting with the transnational concept as we tend to define TNCs as entities beyond and above national borders. However, this is the term used by the UN which reports that 11% of all foreign direct investments (FDIs) are generated by state-owned TNCs in

1.3 Transnationality of Organisations

generated by the TNCs, and the foreign sales, employment and assets of these TNCs have all been increasing recently.

The UNCTAD rankings can be criticised. For example, among the top 100 TNCs in a recent ranking list, the average transnationality score was only 52 %. Hence the question of transnationality of marketing strategies arises and this is elaborated later in this book.

Transnationality Index (TNI) is a simple, perhaps too simplistic, measure. It assumes that spread of sales, assets, and employees over a geography spanning across national borders is an indication of "transnationality" for any given firm (or organisation) from any given country. TNI is calculated as the average of the three ratios: (a) foreign assets to total assets, (b) foreign sales to total sales, (c) foreign employment to total employment. So the mean of these three ratios give us the degree of transnationality (or transnationality index score) of a firm.

Some of the problems with the TNI are known to UNCTAD as acknowledged in their 2007 report: (a) home country size is ignored, (b) sector specifics are overlooked (2007, p. 13). Looking at the top 100 TNCs ranked by UNCTAD and the home countries of these firms can easily show that, for example, the smaller the country of origin, the more likely the firm to score high on TNI score.

For instance, among the top 20 most transnational firms, seven are from relatively small countries whereas there is only one firm from the United States (USA), one of the largest economies in the world. Nevertheless, the problem goes further. Hypothetically, one can imagine that any firm scoring very high on any of these rates (i.e. assets, employees, sales abroad) can also pursue more or less a domestic marketing strategy. At the other extreme, it is also possible to think of, for example, firms with the majority of assets abroad but yet they have a domestic focus.

Moving assets to another country could be simply a means to benefit from cheaper manufacturing costs. Hence it is important to look at the marketing strategy to see whether the organisation follows a transnational marketing strategy or not to determine the 'true transnationality of the organization', which can be simply defined as an optimal balance between the national responsiveness (adaptation) and global integration for efficiency (standardisation).

Transnational marketing strategies seem to be more suitable to certain industries, sectors, and marketing functions as suggested by Bartlett and Beamish (2011, p. 308). In their review of the levels of integration and differentiation at Unilever, the authors argue that chemical businesses are more likely to tend towards standardisation while packaged food businesses are towards high level of adaptation. Hence, detergents stand in the middle and yet value chain activities or business functions differ. While research is likely to be heavily standardised, sales and marketing requires similarly high levels of adaptation to local/national market

---

(Footnote 4 continued)
2010 and it is of a national security concern for many nations due to governance and ownership of these TNCs (UN 2011, p. xiii).

1 Transnationalisation and Transnational Marketing Strategy

Table 1.1 The world's top 100 non-financial TNCs, ranked by foreign assets, 2008

	Corporation	Origin	Industry	Assets	Sales	Staff	TNI
1	Xstrata PLC	UK	Mining and quarrying	94	90	95	93.2
2	ABB Ltd.	Switzerland	Engineering services	81	95	95	90.4
3	Nokia	Finland	Electrical and electronic equipment	91	99	81	90.3
4	Pernod Ricard SA	France	Food, beverages and tobacco	92	90	86	89.1
5	WPP Group Plc	UK	Business services	89	87	91	88.9
6	Vodafone Group Plc	UK	Telecommunications	92	87	87	88.6
7	Linde AG	Germany	Chemicals	90	89	85	88.3
8	Anheuser-Busch Inbev	Netherlands	Food, beverages and tobacco	94	79	90	87.9
9	Anglo American	UK	Mining and quarrying	89	83	90	87.5
10	ArcelorMittal	Luxembrg.	Metal and metal products	96	90	76	87.2
11	Nestlé SA	Switzerland	Food, beverages and tobacco	66	98	97	87.1
12	Air Liquide	France	Chemical/minerals	93	80	88	86.9
13	Liberty Global Inc	USA	Telecommunications	100	100	59	86.2
14	Astrazeneca Plc	UK	Pharmaceuticals	79	94	83	85.4
15	Teva Pharmaceutical	Israel	Pharmaceuticals	74	96	84	84.4
16	Lafarge SA	France	Non-metallic minerals	88	86	79	84.2
17	Volvo AB	Sweden	Motor vehicles	79	95	72	82.3
18	Hutchison Whampoa	Hong Kong	Diversified	81	83	83	82.0
19	Cemex S.A.	Mexico	Non-metalic minerals	89	82	73	81.6
20	BP PLC	UK	Petroleum expl./ref./distr.	83	78	83	81.0
21	Roche Group	Switzerland	Pharmaceuticals	85	99	57	80.3
22	CRH Plc	Ireland	Non-metalic minerals	95	95	49	79.5
23	BAE Systems Plc	UK	Aircraft	89	83	65	78.9
24	Philips Electronics	Netherlands	Electrical and electronic equipment	71	96	69	78.8
25	Schlumberger Ltd	USA	Other consumer services	78	75	78	76.9
26	BG Group Plc	UK	Electricity, gas and water	82	79	67	76.1
27	Total SA	France	Petroleum expl./ref./distr.	86	76	62	74.5
28	SAB Miller	UK	Food, beverages and tobacco	80	67	76	74.4
29	Coca-Cola Company	USA	Food, beverages and tobacco	62	75	86	74.3
30	LVMH	France	Other consumer goods	60	86	74	73.4
31	Diageo Plc	UK	Food, beverages and tobacco	81	87	51	73.0
32	Royal Dutch/Shell Group	UK	Petroleum expl./ref./distr.	79	57	83	73.0
33	Siemens AG	Germany	Electrical and electronic equipment	77	73	69	73.0
34	TeliaSonera AB	Sweden	Telecommunications	86	65	66	72.6
35	De Saint-Gobain SA	France	Non-metallic minerals	72	72	73	72.4
36	Eads NV	France	Aircraft	63	91	63	72.4

(continued)

1.3 Transnationality of Organisations

Table 1.1 (continued)

	Corporation	Origin	Industry	Assets	Sales	Staff	TNI
37	Honda Motor Co Ltd	Japan	Motor vehicles	74	81	61	72.2
38	Unilever	UK	Diversified	60	68	83	70.4
39	Telefonica SA	Spain	Telecommunications	69	64	78	70.3
40	Grupo Ferrovial	Spain	Construction and real estate	81	64	60	68.3
41	Novartis	Switzerland	Pharmaceuticals	56	99	50	68.1
42	ExxonMobil Corporation	USA	Petroleum expl./ref./distr.	71	70	63	67.9
43	Pinault-Printemps Red.	France	Retail and Trade	78	61	63	67.3
44	Holcim AG	Switzerland	Non-metallic minerals	64	62	73	66.3
45	Mitsui & Co Ltd	Japan	Wholesale trade	57	42	95	64.8
46	Vattenfall	Sweden	Electricity, gas and water	55	64	72	63.9
47	Veolia Environnement	France	Utilities	64	60	66	63.2
48	Sony Corporation	Japan	Electrical and electronic equipment	47	76	63	61.8
49	Alcoa	USA	Metal and metal products	71	47	66	61.2
50	IBM	USA	Electrical and electronic equipment	48	65	71	61.1
51	Metro AG	Germany	Retail and Trade	61	61	61	60.9
52	Fiat Spa	Italy	Motor vehicles	48	76	58	60.6
53	Volkswagen Group	Germany	Motor vehicles	53	76	53	60.5
54	National Grid Transco	UK	Utilities	53	66	63	60.4
55	Procter & Gamble	USA	Diversified	47	61	73	60.2
56	Nissan Motor Co Ltd	Japan	Motor vehicles	55	72	51	59.2
57	Sanofi-aventis	France	Pharmaceuticals	50	56	71	59.2
58	Hewlett-Packard	USA	Electrical and electronic equipment	43	69	65	58.9
59	Chevron Corporation	USA	Petroleum expl./ref./distr.	66	56	52	58.1
60	Thyssenkrupp AG	Germany	Metal and metal products	53	64	57	58.1
61	BHP Billiton Group	Australia	Mining and quarrying	44	69	60	57.8
62	Eni Group	Italy	Petroleum expl./ref./distr.	59	60	50	56.4
63	Iberdrola SA	Spain	Utilities	62	54	54	56.4
64	GDF Suez	France	Utilities	51	69	48	56.4
65	Carrefour SA	France	Retail and Trade	39	56	73	56.1
66	BASF AG	Germany	Chemicals	61	56	51	55.9
67	E.On	Germany	Utilities	65	42	61	55.8
68	Glaxosmithkline Plc	UK	Pharmaceuticals	47	63	55	54.8
69	United Technologies	USA	Aircraft	47	52	65	54.7
70	Daimler AG	Germany	Motor vehicles	48	77	39	54.5
71	Ford Motor Company	USA	Motor vehicles	46	59	58	54.3
72	Pfizer Inc	USA	Pharmaceuticals	44	58	61	54.3

(continued)

Table 1.1 (continued)

	Corporation	Origin	Industry	Assets	Sales	Staff	TNI
73	Samsung Electronics	S. Korea	Electrical and electronic equipment	34	81	48	54.2
74	Toyota Motor	Japan	Motor vehicles	57	64	38	52.9
75	General Electric	USA	Electrical and electronic equipment	50	53	53	52.2
76	Johnson & Johnson	USA	Pharmaceuticals	47	49	59	51.8
77	France Telecom	France	Telecommunications	61	47	45	51.0
78	BMW AG	Germany	Motor vehicles	45	80	26	50.3
79	Deutsche Telekom AG	Germany	Telecommunications	55	53	42	50.3
80	Vivendi Universal	France	Telecommunications	45	37	68	50.2
81	Repsol YPF SA	Spain	Petroleum expl./ref./distr.	48	52	51	50.1
82	Kraft Foods Inc.	USA	Food, beverages and tobacco	41	49	60	50.0
83	China Ocean Shipping Gr	China	Transport and storage	77	66	7	49.9
84	General Motors	USA	Motor vehicles	45	49	52	48.7
85	Rio Tinto Plc	UK	Mining and quarrying	53	37	51	47.0
86	Deutsche Post AG	Germany	Transport and storage	8	69	63	46.8
87	Bayer AG	Germany	Pharmaceuticals	35	52	49	45.3
88	Conocophillips	USA	Petroleum expl./ref./distr.	55	31	45	43.4
89	EDP Energias De Portugal	Portugal	Utilities	55	38	37	43.1
90	Electricite De France	France	Utilities	48	47	32	42.2
91	Sumitomo Corporation	Japan	Wholesale trade	37	51	37	42.0
92	RWE Group	Germany	Utilities	41	37	40	39.7
93	Hyundai Motor Company	S. Korea	Motor vehicles	35	47	28	36.5
94	Statoil Asa	Norway	Petroleum expl./ref./distr.	46	24	39	36.4
95	Marubeni Corporation	Japan	Wholesale trade	52	35	17	34.6
96	Mitsubishi Corporation	Japan	Wholesale trade	53	11	30	31.3
97	Wal-Mart Stores	USA	Retail and Trade	38	25	31	31.2
98	Hitachi Ltd	Japan	Electrical and electronic equipment	25	33	35	31.2
99	Petronas - Petroliam	Malaysia	Petroleum expl./ref./distr.	27	42	20	29.6
100	CITIC Group	China	Diversified	18	24	20	21.0

Source UNCTAD (2010) World Investment Report

needs. Marketing as a business function tend to be more responsive to national differences. This therefore requires more adaptation. However, within marketing function, tasks such as product policies tend to be standardised; whereas promotion and advertising tasks crave a high level of adaptation. The dominance of pharmaceutical, chemical, petroleum, and energy companies in the Top 100 TNCs list is supportive of this argument. At the same time, it is also fair to say that transnationalism is not for every business and every business function. Transnational approach requires a rather fine-tuned attitude and approach when setting up strategies.

Another hypothetical situation against the UNCTAD's definition of transnationality is related to the increased human mobility around the world. Many organisations have a very transnational body of staff who can offer input from different backgrounds and experiences and are based in one country. Here the point is to show that mobility and dispersal of staff is not a necessary condition for pursuing transnational strategies.[5] Having a multi-culturally mixed body of employees can enable these firms to develop transnational strategies without extensive investment abroad. However, marketing orientation should also be taken into account when determining the transnationality of the firms or organisations.

In their best seller text book, Keegan and Green imply, incorrectly, that global and transnational companies are same as both adopt geocentric orientation (2008, pp. 22 and 611). Obviously this is not correct, but, what is valuable in their account is that they argue transnational companies serve global markets while utilizing global supply chains and often have a blurred national identity; hence they are characterized as "stateless" (2008, p. 23). They also emphasise that the distinguishing factor between "international or multinational companies" and transnational ones is the "mind-set" but it only refers to the use of market research.

What we need to consider is to what extent is a *transnational mentality* embedded in the marketing approach, a building block of a transnational marketing organisation. Cross-border production efficiencies, innovation and knowledge creation as well as sharing experiences and knowledge are essential for a successful transnational organisation. Thus, the organisation and its parts will see an exponential growth of information and knowledge sharing taking place (Stonehouse et al. 2004, p. 170; Quinn 1992, p. 254). As the ultimate strategy in the matrix of global, multi-domestic and domestic options, businesses following a transnational strategy need to have all their participating firms behaving as a collective learning organisation to achieve global efficiency and local/national responsiveness at the same time.

Transnational mentality has been forced upon multinational organisations. For example, host country governments have demanded more local involvement in their operations such as technology transfers and local content requirements. On the other hand, as mentioned earlier, the customers, despite increasing mobility and connectedness across the world remained as locals and nationals with differences in tastes and preferences. Bartlett and Beamish called this "the return of *national* into terminology" while maintaining "competitive effectiveness and economic efficiency, as indicated by the prefix *trans*" (2011, p. 13). Thus such

---

[5] When we discuss transnational consumers and transnational mobiles we will elaborate the relevance of human mobility further.

organisations are superior to others with global mentality, multinational mentality, or international mentality.[6]

The transnational organisation is able to develop and naturally benefit from multiple diverse internal perspectives while having distributed, and yet independent, assets and management capabilities internationally and at the same time having and robust flexible integrative process (Bartlett and Beamish 2011, p. 305). Consequently the transnational marketing organisation would not suffer from the inability of global organisation to respond to local market needs due to lack of resources and organisational structures whilst also avoiding the inefficiencies due to fragmented activities of a classic multinational company. Organisations with transnational mentality need to adopt strategies in line at every level and in every function. This includes having transnational staff members in the board room, in project teams, involved in cross-country initiatives as well as having repatriation and rotation programmes to facilitate cross-border exchanges within the organisation.[7] As such "the transnational is characterised by its legitimization of multidimensional perspectives, its distributed and interdependent capabilities, and its flexible integrative processes. It is a model that is increasingly becoming mainstream" (Bartlett and Beamish 2011, p. 314). The transnational marketing organisation enables more flexibility and effective decision making within a system where global activities are integrated and interdependent involving headquarters and subsidiaries in other countries. Bartlett and Ghoshal warn here that understanding of cultural differences and patience are key success factors in a transnational organisation as the teams involve people with entirely different cultural backgrounds.

Nevertheless, the transnationality of a firm/organisation is probably only measured accurately when the transnationality of their marketing strategy is also taken into account. In the next section, after defining *transnational marketing*, the transnationality of marketing strategy and how it moderates the transnationality of the firm will be elaborated with examples from the UNCTAD's TNI ranking list.

1.4 Transnational Marketing and Transnational Marketing Strategy

The UNCTAD's transnationality index is in need of improvement by integration of transnationality of marketing strategy into the formula. Today Levitt's (1983) globalisation era, marked by a shift towards standardisation of products and

---

[6] For details of these three mentalities see Bartlett and Beamish (2011, pp. 11–13).

[7] However, there are challenges and barriers to such high level of staff mobility and engagement, possibly affecting larger and smaller enterprises at differing degrees. Existing regulations privilege the transnationally mobility of capital and owners of the mobile capital while not so the interests of 'stakeholders' who are to an extent tied to a spatially fixed and localised labour process (Overbeek et al. 2007, p. 213).

convergence of demand across the world, has gone. The "stateless" organisation now needs to address often very national and local varied customer needs, wants and desires while also tackling with legal boundaries and ensuring optimal efficiencies in response to national and local requirements, demands and desires. Thus, "think global, act local" becomes a very popular and perhaps overused cliché. Nevertheless, this is the wavelength I pitch the concepts of transnational marketing and transnational consumers.

Transnational marketing is a new concept in the literature of consumer behaviour and marketing strategy. Nonetheless, there is a good number of studies on transnational firms, organizations and corporations, and contracts (Smith and Eade 2008; Ietto-Gillies 2005; Pitelis and Sugden 2000; Kneen 2002; Chatterjee 1996; Lall 1993; Jones 1993). In many marketing texts and articles, 'transnational marketing' has been mentioned but not really elaborated and defined. Well known texts, such as *Transnational Management* by Bartlett and colleagues is no exception to such lack of depth. It does only briefly introduce the *transnationality index* and differentiates types of organisations but, to an extent, leaves transnational marketing undefined. In some other works of Bartlett, a few more ideas are added about the 'transnational' but still the term is used rather confusingly, referring strongly to the 'global' description. It is pretty common that the two terms are used interchangeably which implies that global and transnational are almost the same we beg to differ.

To define what "Transnational" may mean in marketing, I would like to revisit the definitions of four stages in a firm's marketing internationalisation. Very few international marketing and business texts refer to international, multinational, global, and transnational as four strategy options (Mooradian et al. 2012, p. 185) or phases or stages in firm's internationalisation (Ghauri and Cateora 2006, pp. 17–19; Cherunilam, 2010, p. 18) or "gradual evolution" (Bartlett and Beamish, 2011, p. 11).

International Marketing is the performance of business activities designed to plan, price, promote and direct the flow of a company's goods and services to consumers or users in more than one nation for a profit. The only difference between the definitions of domestic marketing and international marketing is that, in the latter case, marketing activities take place in more than one country (Cateora and Graham 2007). This is very similar to what Mooradian et al. (2012) call an international marketing strategy where the emphasis is on the centralisation of functions and a standardised marketing mix.

Multinational Marketing is defined as companies treat that each foreign market as separate and distinct, developing differentiated products and marketing strategies specifically for each market (Albaum and Duerr 2008, pp. 14, 15, 688). On the other hand, Usunier and Lee (2005, p. 218), like many others, use the term *Multidomestic* referring to separate marketing strategies pursued in different national markets. The focus here is on substantial differences in different national markets and customised marketing mixes offered in each; or "multimix" strategies employed (Mooradian et al. 2012, p. 186).

Global Marketing was defined as a strategy where firms treat the entire world as a single market and sell the same product in the same way everywhere (Levitt 1983). It is also about the firm's commitment to coordinate its marketing activities across national boundaries in order to find and satisfy global customer needs better than the competition (Hollensen 2007, p. 7). Albaum and Duerr defines *Global Marketer* as "companies that are using an integrated worldwide marketing strategy based on consistent brand selling for their products, making only minor changes required by differing markets" (2008, pp. 14, 686).

Transnational Marketing or transnational marketing strategy requires a rather delicate balance and approach where the motto is as much standardisation as possible and as much on adaptation as needed. The emergence of a *Transnational Model* can be dated back to the end of the 1980s when Bartlett and Ghoshal argued that by then, many internationally oriented companies adopted the transnational model (Barlett and Ghoshal 1989). Accordingly, companies are expected to leverage their capabilities across borders and transfer best practices to achieve global economies and respond to the local market conditions (Hollensen 2007, p. 648). This is possible with a transnational organization, in contrast to its multinational, international or global counterparts. It is an organisation that "builds and legitimises multiple diverse internal perspectives able to sense the complex environmental demands and opportunities; its physical assets and management capabilities are distributed internationally but are interdependent; and it has developed a robust and flexible internal integrative process" (Bartlett and Ghoshal 2000, p. 512).

Transnational marketing strategy refers to a global marketing strategy and multidomestic marketing strategy with a focus on internal efficiency through global integration of marketing programmes. In such a strategic approach, decision making may be centralized to offer standardized products and services across national boundaries without compromising the external flexibility allowing adaptation of products and services to local demands (Wasilewski 2002, p. 127).

Thus *Transnational Marketing* can be defined as *understanding and addressing customer needs, wants and desires in their own countries of residence and beyond and in borderless cultural contexts with the help of synergies emerging across national boundaries and transfer of expertise and advantages shared between markets where the organization operates transnationally (i.e. functions based in two or more countries) with a transnational mentality supported by transnational organization structures and without compromising the sustainability of any target markets and resource environment offering satisfactory exchanges between the parties involved.*

This definition takes into account basics of marketing while also integrating concerns about sustainability and the need for an appropriate organisational structure to draw upon advantages and synergies emerging from different markets. At this point, to wrap up the transnational marketing definition, it is useful to look into mentality differences in marketing proposed by Bartlett and Beamish (2011).

The Ethnocentric-Polycentric-Regiocentric-Geocentric (EPRG) schema has been used and discussed widely since the 1970s in distinguishing marketing orientations ranging from *ethnocentric to geocentric*, where the former is characterised by a managerial perception viewing "domestic techniques and personnel as superior to foreign" while the latter is described as "a world orientation" (Wind et al. 1973, pp. 14, 15). Ghauri and Cateora (2006, p. 21) present the same framework and emphasize the need for different marketing mixes in different countries, but their argument remain short of the *transnational orientation*, if I may call it.

Bartlett and Beamish (2011) propose a model of gradual evolution of strategic mentality imposed by the development of a firms' engagement in international marketing. According to them, a combination of host country governments' growing demands, customers' rejection of homogenized products, and economic and political volatility forced firms to adjust their *global mentality,* as embodied in Levitt's famous "the same thing, the same way, everywhere" (1983, p. 93), to the localizing forces (Bartlett and Beamish 2011, pp. 12, 13). Hence internationalised firms feel the urge to be responsive to local market while continuing with their pursuit of global-scale competitive efficiency simultaneously. Transnational mentality then, in contrast to the global model, recognizes the importance of flexible and responsive country-level operations.

In Table 1.2, the main differences between these mentalities and orientations are summarised. Nevertheless, it is important to recognize that despite the likely gradual development of an internationalisation strategy, many firms leapfrog skipping one or more of the stages proposed in the process. Transnational marketing orientation is classified as the ultimate form of a dynamic and successful firm benefiting from cross-border synergies and exchanges while also benefiting from some global integration efficiencies and maintaining a virtually stateless organisation where country markets are researched continuously. As local variation in needs, wants and desires as well as in the context has to be addressed, economies of scale may be difficult to achieve but customer satisfaction is likely to be high. One downside of transnational strategy is the need for relatively complex organisational structures, which ultimately increase management costs.

Is the degree of transnationality of the firm, or the degree of transnationality of marketing strategy or having a transnational mentality that is important? Perhaps it is all of these when it comes to devising a marketing strategy, a marketing plan involving various marketing mix decisions. In the next section, the transnationality of the organisation is revisited with reference to the transnationality of firms' marketing strategy drawing upon a small-scale survey conducted in 2011.

Identifying the level of transnationality in an organisation by using the tools and formulas described above do not help marketers in the increasingly competitive and transnational marketing environment. For instance, in theory, it is possible that a firm may have its staff spread across many countries and have production facilities in several countries and the majority of sales recorded in many countries, while applying a perfectly standardised marketing strategy. Yet this firm does not necessarily pursue transnational marketing strategies. We believe the true transnationality of a firm comes from a combination of the above criteria (i.e. sales, staff, assets) and the ways in which transnationality is reflected in its marketing

Table 1.2 Marketing strategy by the type of orientation

Domestic	*Advantages*
Marketing mix is developed solely for the domestic market; no interest in internationalisation	Consistency in portfolio
	Simple organisation and effective control
	Disadvantages
	Ignorant of foreign market opportunities
	Unexploited economies of scale
International/ethnocentric	*Advantages*
Marketing mix developed for the domestic market and subsequently marketed abroad with no adjustment; home country is assumed to be superior to the rest of the world; products are believed to be sold everywhere without adaptation	Consistency in portfolio
	Simple organisation and effective control
	Economies of scale
	Domestic market is protected
	Disadvantages
	Differences in markets including customers, environment and competition is ignored
	Not exploiting potential benefits from destination markets in terms or resources and synergies
	Decisions made ad hoc and in an opportunistic manner
	Valuable managerial knowledge and experience in local markets unnoticed
Multinational/polycentric	*Advantages*
A different marketing mix developed for each market; assumes that each country market is unique; localized approach where products are adapted to each market along with customised multiple and nationally responsive strategies	Differences in markets including customers, environment and competition is acknowledged
	Full exploitation of local markets through adaptation
	Flexible approach and strategies
	Disadvantages
	Little economies of scale
	Inconsistent portfolio
	Duplication of efforts; hence inflating marketing costs
	Limited control over subsidiaries
Global/regiocentric and geocentric[a]	*Advantages*
Firms offer a single marketing mix to sell "the same thing, the same way, everywhere" (Levitt 1983); may serve the world from a single country and source globally; most strategic decisions and research and development are handled at the headquarters	High level of centralised control and decision making
	Cost advantages through integrated global strategies
	High economies of scale
	Standardised, consistent portfolio and brands
	Disadvantages
	Assumes homogeneity in national markets and tastes
	Ignores national differences

(continued)

1.4 Transnational Marketing and Transnational Marketing Strategy

Table 1.2 (continued)

Transnational	Advantages
Ultimate form of a dynamic and successful international/multinational firm[b]; recognizes national differences and yet strives to achieve efficiency through global integration; stateless marketing organisation; decisions are based on continuous market research;	High level of control and partly de-centralised decision making involving cross-country input back and forth
	Cost advantages through integrated global strategies
	Moderate economies of scale
	Cross-border adaptations and customisations
	Benefiting from synergies and advantages created at national level and shared transnationally
	Resources and activities are dispersed but specialised to achieve efficiency and flexibility
	Disadvantages
	Involves complex organisational structures
	Can be costly in marketing and organisation but it is balanced with advantages gained overall from adaptation, innovation across the board

[a] Regiocentric and geocentric strategies are based on very similar assumptions where regiocentric is also similar to polycentric type when a firm operates in multiple regions globally while altering the marketing mix for each broad region

[b] Cherunilam argues that "transnational is used to define the ultimate phase in development of international firm" (2010, p. 19)

strategy. This need for transnational marketing strategy arises from the fact that transnational problems cannot be solved by national teams and national perspectives alone. For example, the governance approach argues that national civil societal and governmental controls should be replaced by transnational NGOs to monitor and sanction irresponsible business behaviour (Nolke and Perry 2007, p. 126). One such NGO is *International Baby Food Action Network* who run a strong campaign against Nestle[8] over baby milk formula product in India. The challenge was that baby milk formula was designed to be used with clean water while in the target country water was mostly contaminated, thus making the product impractical. The campaign forced the company to become more responsive to the Indian marketing environment and adjust the overall marketing strategy in that part of their transnational network. The key feature to note here is that the protesting NGOs are also following transnational strategies.[9]

---

[8] Nestle was one of the most transnational company ranked second on UNCTAD's 2007 transnationality index ranking (UN 2007).

[9] One leading NGO still pursue boycotting Nestle (see www.babymilkaction.org) while also being part of a transnational alliance of over 200 NGOs across the world: International Baby Food Action Network (IBFAN: http://www.ibfan.org/).

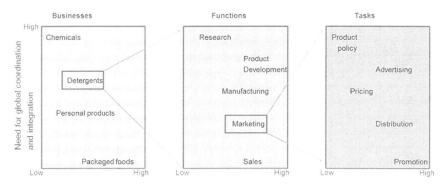

Fig. 1.1 Global integration versus national responsiveness needs. *Source* Bartlett and Beamish (2011, p. 308) based on a model first developed by Prahalad and Doz (1987)

Bartlett and Ghoshal (1989) can be considered as pioneers of transnationalism in management strategy. They have defined *transnational* as configuration, control and coordination of global businesses in pursuit of global competitiveness without sacrificing local/national adaptation and customised as required for strategy and structures. Later Stonehouse et al. (2004, p. 16) described transnational strategy as "one that combines a global configuration and co-ordination of business activities with local responsiveness, based on continuous organisational learning, and consists of: global knowledge-based core competences giving access to global markets; extensive participation in major world markets; global configuration of value-adding activities which exploits both national similarities and differences; global co-ordination and integration of activities; local responsiveness where required; differentiated structure and organisation". This is similar to Yip's *total global strategy* (1992, p. 4) where a transnational strategy is used interchangeably with global strategy and simplified as taking advantage of both global and local conditions through a differentiated, rather than standardised, approach to business (Stonehouse et al. 2004, p. 17). Nevertheless, over the 1990s, an understanding of 'transnational strategy', referring to efficiency gains allowing scale economies while benefiting from the advantages of national responsiveness, has emerged.

As shown in Fig. 1.1, a transnational approach is more likely in certain industries and more applicable to certain business functions, marketing is inclined to be more nationally and/or locally responsive. There again, marketing mix decisions concerning the mix components may not allow same level of efficiencies and responsiveness. For example, the use of brands *Elvital* in Germany and *Elseve* in France are both making a reference to the meaning of *vital* and *seve*. However, probably because the word does not have a meaning in Hungarian, in the adverts used in Hungary for the very same *Elseve*, the emphasis is rather on the place of origin: "From L'Oreal from Paris". In this case, the core benefit and core product is the same and thus offers a high level of standardisation (i.e. global integration-efficiency) while the advertising is differentiated across countries as there is higher need for national responsiveness. For example, advertising copy and communication materials need to be translated; channels used to reach the target customers have to be adjusted to the local infrastructure.

Wasilevski (2001) tested the I-R (integration-responsiveness) framework by assessing the six areas of international marketing strategy on a 7-point Likert scale. His focus was on the marketing success of strategic business units (SBUs) and based on managers' self-reporting from 113 US-based MNCs. He concludes that companies with more transnational marketing strategy are likely to be more successful in the market. Adopting his model, we have investigated the transnationality of marketing strategies in SBUs of TNCs; basically asked questions about the degree of customisation and of standardisation in each of the four marketing mix areas as was done by Wasilevski (2001).

His claim that transnational strategy breeds success surely needs some more empirical testing. However, the measurement of transnationality of the strategy by managers' perception of their firms' marketing strategy, including some marketing mix areas, seems useful for our study. Thus, a very similar methodology is used here to see whether the companies in the list of top 50 TNCs do pursue transnational marketing strategies or not. It is possible to have companies which might be classified as "transnational" according to the spatial spread of their sales, employees and assets but yet pursuing either global or domestic strategies. These can be rare cases but to improve the definition, there is value in understanding whether their marketing strategies (as perceived by their managers) are also transnational.

For this purpose, we have randomly selected 25 companies from the top 50 TNCs listed in the UNCTAD ranking. We have emailed a short questionnaire with 16 questions to 114 SBU managers in these companies. Companies were randomly chosen from UNCTAD's 2008 transnationality index ranking list. Our survey yielded 23 complete questionnaires (16 % response rate).[10] The questionnaire included some background questions about the respondent's role in the company and geographical focus if any. The first six questions focused on whether the SBU's strategy aims to standardise products, pricing, promotion, distribution, product development, overall standardised (or global) approach to country markets. The second set of questions asked opinion on whether the SBU's strategy aims to tailor products, differentiate pricing, customize advertising, adjust distribution, introduce new products selectively, and pay attention to uniqueness of country markets.

As shown in Table 1.3, average transnationality scores in our survey are in line with the expectations and with the UNCTAD rankings. Most firms scored high on both integration and responsiveness scales. Unilever, Oriflame, Nestle and few others score high in transnationality whilst some others mainly due to the

---

[10] I would like to thank Martina Drennow who conducted the questionnaire survey as part of her dissertation research.

Table 1.3 Average scores: transnationality, integration, responsiveness

Brands-SBUs	Integration	Responsiveness	TransIndex
Frost & Sullivan	5.67	5.00	5.33
Unilever-Clear	5.00	5.50	5.25
Oriflame	5.50	5.00	5.25
Unilever-Clear	5.83	4.50	5.17
Nestlé	4.00	5.83	4.92
iZettle	4.67	5.17	4.92
Oriflame-Cosmetics	5.00	4.83	4.92
Mercedes-Benz	4.33	5.33	4.83
Unilever-Sunsilk	4.50	5.17	4.83
Mindshare-Mazda	4.17	5.33	4.75
MediaEdge CIA	4.33	4.83	4.58
BAT-Lucky Strike	5.67	3.50	4.58
Procter & Gamble	5.00	4.00	4.50
Unilever-Clear	5.17	3.58	4.38
Unilever-Ponds	3.00	5.67	4.33
Preem AB	6.17	2.50	4.33
H&M	6.17	2.33	4.25
LVMH	5.17	2.83	4.00
Orkla	1.83	5.67	3.75
MONTBLANC International	4.83	2.50	3.67
Danone	2.33	4.83	3.58
Telia Sonera	2.83	3.83	3.33
Carat	2.50	4.00	3.25

characteristics of their products and markets scored quite low. For example, Danone, marketing dairy products such as yoghurt, has to pay more attention to national markets and local needs whereas BAT's Lucky Strike needed less of that. Unilever's Pond's also placed more emphasis on national differences for its skin care products whereas for Moët Hennessy Louis Vuitton's (LVMH) Champagnes' a global emphasis was more important and appropriate. Hence following the argument by Bartlett and Beamish, it is possible to claim that products, industries, and markets play a role in determining the need for standardisation and adaption in designing transnational marketing strategies.

When the integration and responsiveness scores mapped, it was possible to locate marketing strategies in our matrix to illustrate the level of transnationality of their marketing strategies against each other (Fig. 1.2). It is clear that Frost & Sullivan, a business consultancy firm with higher flexibility with tailoring the service offering as well as possible efficiencies, scored high on both scales and appear closest to the transnational strategy on the top right corner. On the other hand, two fashion brands, H&M and LVMH score high on global integration but low on adaptation which is mainly due to the nature of products they offer, fashion and luxury, which in both cases are more valuable when standardised. Thus,

1.4 Transnational Marketing and Transnational Marketing Strategy

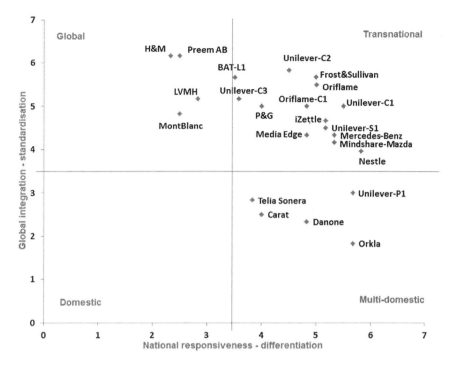

Fig. 1.2 Transnationality of marketing strategies

geographical spread of assets, employees, and sales across national borders does not necessarily mean transnationality in terms of marketing strategy.

All the firms we analysed are among the top 100 TNCs but, as seen from the Fig. 1.2, some of them have marketing strategies perceived to be more transnational than others. As mentioned earlier, one main reason for this variation is distinct characteristics of sectors these firms operate and products and services they offer.

Organisations have to recognise these differences and address them by adjusting their marketing strategies. Yet they must also address the differences in consumer behaviour and consumer characteristics. The next chapter is focusing on the transnational consumers and mobility and movement as variables to be used in segmenting markets.

References

Albaum, G., & Duerr, E. (2008). *International marketing and export management.* Harlow, UK: Pearson Education.

Bartlett, C. A., & Beamish, P. W. (2011). *Transnational management: Text, readings, and cases in cross-border management.* Burr Ridge, IL: Irwin McGraw-Hill.

Bartlett, C. A., & Ghoshal, S. (1989). *Managing across borders: The transnational solution*. Boston, MA: Harvard Business School Press.

Bartlett, C. A., & Ghoshal, S. (2000). *Transnational management: Text, cases and readings in cross-border management* (3rd ed.). Boston, MA: McGraw-Hill.

Basch, L. G., Schiller, N. G., & Blanc-Szanton, C. (1994). *Nations unbound: Transnational projects, post-colonial predicaments, and de-territorialization of nation-states*. Langhorne, PA: Gordon and Breach.

Bauman, Z. (1995). Searching for a centre that holds. In M. Featherstone, S. Lash, & R. Robertson (Eds.), *Global modernities* (pp. 140–54). London: Sage.

Burton, D. (2005). Marketing theory matters. *British Journal of Management, 16*(1), 5–18.

Cateora, P. R., & Graham, J. L. (2007). *International marketing*. New York: McGraw-Hill.

Chatterjee, C. (1996). *Legal aspects of transnational marketing and sales contracts*. London: Cavendish Pub.

Cherunilam, F. (2010). *International business, text and cases*: New Delhi, India: PHI.

Deloitte. (2012). *Strategic moves 2012: The global mobility island*. Deloitte. http://www.deloitte.com/view/en_GX/global/services/consulting/human-capital/strategic-moves/index.htm?id=gx:th:SM12.

Foner, N. (1997). What's new about transnationalism? New York immigrants today and at the turn of the century. *Diaspora, 6*, 355–375.

Ghauri, P. N., & Cateora, P. (2006). *International marketing* (2nd ed.). London: McGraw-Hill.

Giddens, A. (1997). *Sociology* (3rd ed.). Cambridge, UK: Polity.

Grewal, I., & Kaplan, C. (Eds.). (1994). *Scattered hegemonies: Postmodernity and transnational feminist practices*. Minneapolis, MN: University of Minnesota Press.

Hall, R., & Biersteker, T. (Eds.). (2002). *The emergence of private authority in global governance*. Cambridge: Cambridge University Press.

Harzing, A. (2000). An empirical test and extension of the Bartlett and Ghoshal typology of multinational companies. *Journal of International Business Studies, 31*(1), 101–120.

Hearn, J. (2004). Tracking 'the Transnational': Studying transnational organizations and managements, and the management of cohesion. *Culture and Organization, 10*(4), 273–290.

Hollensen, S. (2007). *Global marketing: A decision-oriented approach*. Harlow, UK: Prentice Hall.

Ietto-Gillies, G. (2005). *Transnational corporations and international production*. Cheltenham, UK: Edward-Elgar.

Jackson, P., Crang, P., & Dwyer, C. (Eds.). (2004). *Transnational spaces*. London: Routledge.

Jones, G. (Ed.). (1993). *Transnational corporations: A historical perspective* (Vol. 2). London: Taylor & Francis.

Kearney, M. (1995). The local and the global: The anthropology of globalization and transnationalism. *Annual Review of Anthropology, 24*, 547–565.

Keegan, W. J., & Green, M. C. (2008). *Global marketing* (5th ed.). Upper Saddle River, NJ: Pearson Prentice Hall.

Kimmitt, R., Garay, M., & Allen, D. (2010). Money and borders: Cross-border investments in a changing global market place. *Deloitte Review, 6*, 56–69.

Kneen, B. (2002). *Invisible giant: Cargill and its transnational strategies*. London: Pluto Press.

Lall, S. (Ed.). (1993). *Transnational corporations and economic development*. London: Routledge.

Levitt, T. (1983). The globalisation of markets. *Harvard Business Review, 61*(3), 92–102.

Miller, D. (Ed.). (1995). *Worlds apart: Modernity through the prism of the local*. London: Routledge.

Miller, D. (1997). *Capitalism: An ethnographic approach*. Oxford: Berg.

Mooradian, T. A., Matzler, K., & Ring, L. J. (2012). *Strategic marketing*. Upper Saddle River, NJ: Pearson Prentice Hall.

Nölke, A., & Perry, J. (2007). Coordination service firms and the erosion of Rhenish capitalism. In H. Overbeek, B. van Apeldoorn, & A. Nölke (Eds.), *The transnational politics of corporate governance regulation* (pp. 121–136). Oxon, UK: Routledge.

References

Overbeek, H, van Apeldoorn, B., & Nölke, A. (Eds.). (2007). *The transnational politics of corporate governance regulation.* Oxon, UK: Routledge.

Parhizgar, K. D. (1999). Globalisation of multicultural management. *Journal of Transnational Management, 3*(4), 1–23.

Pitelis, C. N., & Sugden, R. (Eds.). (2000). *The nature of the transnational firm.* London: Routledge.

Prahalad, C. K., & Doz, Y. (1987). *The multinational mission.* New York: The Free Press.

Quinn, J. B. (1992). *The intelligent enterprise.* New York: Free Press.

Simon-Miller, F. (1986). World marketing: Going global or acting local? Five expert viewpoints. *Journal of Consumer Marketing, 3*(2), 5–7.

Smith, M. P., & Eade, J. (Eds.). (2008). *Transnational ties: Cities, migrations, and identities.* New Brunswick, NJ: Transaction Pub.

Stonehouse, G., Campbell, D., Hamill, J., & Purdie, T. (2004). *Global and transnational business: strategy and management.* Chichester, UK: John Wiley and Sons.

Tedlow, R. S., & Abdelal, R. (2004). Theodore Levitt's 'The Globalization of Markets': An evaluation after two decades. In J. A. Quelch & R. Deshpandé (Eds.), *The global market: Developing a strategy to manage across borders* (pp. 11–30). San Francisco, CA: Jossey-Bass.

UNCTAD (United Nations). (1991). *World Investment Report 1991. The triad in foreign direct investment.* New York: UNCTAD (United Nations).

UNCTAD (United Nations). (2007). *World Investment Report 2007. Transnational corporations, extractive industries and development.* New York: UNCTAD (United Nations).

UNCTAD (United Nations). (2010). *World Investment Prospects Survey 2010–2012.* New York: UNCTAD (United Nations).

UNCTAD (United Nations). (2011). *World Investment Report 2011.* New York: UNCTAD (United Nations).

Usunier, J. C., & Lee, J. A. (2005). *Marketing across cultures.* Harlow, UK: Pearson Education.

Van Apeldoorn, B., & Horn, L. (2007). The marketisation of European corporate control: A critical political economy perspective. *New Political Economy, 12*(2), 211–235.

Vertovec, S. (2004). Transnationalism. In P. Jackson, P. Crang, & C. Dwyer (Eds.), *Transnational spaces* (p. ii). London: Routledge.

Vliegenthart, A., & Overbeek, H. (2007). Corporate governance regulation in East Central Europe: The role of transnational forces. In H. Overbeek, B. van Apeldoorn, & A. Nölke (Eds.), *The transnational politics of corporate governance regulation* (pp. 177–198). Oxon, UK: Routledge.

Wasilewski, N. (2001). The pursuit of transnational strategies. Paper presented at Academy of Business and Administrative Sciences, July 23–25, Belgium. Available at: http://www.sba.muohio.edu/abas/2001/brussels/proceedings.html.

Wasilewski, N. (2002). An empirical study of the desirability and challenges of implementing transnational marketing strategies. *Advances in Competitiveness Research, 10*(1), 123–149.

Wigger, A. (2007). Towards a market-based approach: The privatization and microeconomization of EU antitrust law enforcement. In H. Overbeek, B. van Apeldoorn, & A. Nölke (Eds.), *The transnational politics of corporate governance regulation* (pp. 98–118). Oxon, UK: Routledge.

Webster's (1988) *Webster's Dictionary* (9th ed.). Springfield, MA: Merriam-Webster Inc.

Wind, Y., Douglas, S. P., & Perlmutter, H. V. (1973). Guidelines for developing international marketing strategies. *Journal of Marketing, 37*(2), 14–23.

Yip, G. S. (1992). *Total global strategy: Managing for worldwide competitive advantage.* Eaglewood Cliffs, NJ: Prentice Hall.

Chapter 2
Transnationals: Transnational Consumers and Transnational Mobile Consumers

The subheading above may appear confusing but the two terms are used on purpose to provoke debate on the possibility of having two broader segments relating to the transnational marketing era. Levitt (1983) was expecting an ultimate convergence of tastes, wants and desires which would make all of us more or less "global consumers". As known to marketing scholars and practitioners, there are global consumer segments who are believed to consume similar things in a similar way. However, the rise of a global culture does not mean though, consumers share the same values and tastes everywhere, but that they participate in a shared conversation (Holt et al. 2004, p. 2). However, increasingly more nuances are being discovered among these so-called global consumers and it seems mainly due to a simple fact that these consumers share a lot but yet remain as nationals and locals to an extent. The *transnationals* introduced in this brief are different from these *globals* and *locals* in terms of their connectedness and mobility.

New technologies and increasing prosperity, coinciding with relatively inexpensive transportation, has facilitated an increased connectivity among governments, firms, and more importantly individuals, as consumers. Transnational consumers are those people who understand, perceive and behave in a framework transcending the national and local (socio-cultural, political, economic, and technological) reference points. They are often linked to more than one national framework and/or referring to such behaviour patterns beyond any national framework. Therefore, we have those consumers who are not mobile but connected transnationally as well as others who are spatially mobile, spending substantial periods abroad or on travelling or moved abroad, and yet stay in touch with the countries of origin and countries of transit. Hence the *transnationals* as a consumer segment can be examined in two sub-groups: (i) *transnationals* (or borderless non-mobiles) and (ii) *transnational mobiles* (or borderless mobiles).[1]

---

[1] An earlier conceptualization of the term can be found in Sirkeci and Mannix (2009 and 2010). Figueiredo and Cayla later presented a similar concept in a conference paper (2012).

I. Sirkeci, *Transnational Marketing and Transnational Consumers*,
SpringerBriefs in Business, DOI: 10.1007/978-3-642-36775-5_2,
© The Author(s) 2013

It is important to underline here that to be "transnational", mobility is not essential. The transnational outlook, connectedness, being part of such networks spanning across national borders can influence consumption patterns. Transnational [non-mobile] consumers are the ones who are *transnationally oriented*.[2]

Mobility and movement have not been considered among marketing segmentation variables despite some growing literature on immigrant consumers. Nevertheless, people, or consumers, have always been mobile and contemporary consumer societies are more mobile than ever. Perhaps early mobile groups such as Pilgrims or Free Masons[3] appearing as an imagined community in the fifteenth Century can be called early transnational mobile consumers as they have developed and shown patterns of behaviour beyond any single national cultural reference points and with some "gestures and signs of recognition allowing them to gain confidence and credit of counterparts abroad" (Pijl 1998, p. 99). However, some national cultural set of references are likely to be found dominant in these mobile individuals' and groups perceptions and behaviour.

Transnational consumers, as is the case with transnational firms, can be confused with the *globals*. Globals or global consumers can be defined as those whose social and cultural differences are overshadowed by their similarities in terms of psychological consumer tendencies, mainly focusing on attitudes in the market and towards firms, brands, and products (See Cleveland and Laroche 2007; Singh et al. 2006; Holt et al. 2004; Firat 1997). Holt et al. (2004, p. 5) identify four global consumer segments: Global citizens, global dreamers, antiglobals, and global agnostics. These are defined by their perceptions of transnational companies with no reference to consumers' own characteristics, and certainly not mentioning their connectedness and mobility levels. However, what Culley and Hudson (2010) refers to as "fertility tourists or global consumers" would fall among our transnational mobiles because mobility appears to be a defining characteristic.

We can link transnational consumers to the globalization of the marketplace, which is a process influencing the cultural characteristics of people around the world. In due course, "powerful forces such as capitalism, global transport, communications, marketing and advertising, and transnational cosmopolitanism are interacting to dissolve the boundaries across national cultures and economies" (Cleveland and Laroche 2007, p. 249). It is difficult to claim that this process is creating a homogeneous global consumer culture. However this process is blurring the national and cultural boundaries and borders and thus paving way for transnational consumer practices.

---

[2] In a different context, Derne (2008) refers to "transnationally oriented" family members.

[3] Pijl (1998, p. 99) calls them "transnational classes".

2.1 Connectedness and the Consumer E-Geography

Konrad (1984) and Hannerz (1992) referred to intellectuals "without boundaries," who are "at home in the cultures of other peoples as well as in their own. They keep track of what is happening in various places.... They have friends all over the world.... They fly to visit one another as easily as their counterparts 200 years ago rode to the next town to exchange ideas" (Konrad 1984, pp. 208–209).

'Transnationally connected intellectuals' may or may not be adequately large or appealing as a segment, but the internet and wireless technologies have changed the nature and speed people connect with each other while also changing the marketing and marketing environment for good. For our discussion here, the most important influence of internet has been the level of connectedness among consumers around the world. Often it is referred to as "hyperconnectivity" enabling global customer and talent markets, making geographic distances and national borders almost irrelevant. Some so-called revolutions have been organized, or at least facilitated, via tweets and facebook sharing. There is now a generation who have always had the internet in their world. According to the International Telecommunications Union,[4] internet penetration rates are increasing rapidly around the world: More than 3 quarters of people in North America, two-thirds of Europe and Australasia have access to internet. Percentages of internet users in Africa grew over 36 times in the last decade or so whilst it grew 26 times in the Middle East. In China, internet user numbers jumped from about 22 million to over 530 million in the same period. In some European countries such as Norway and Iceland nearly all individuals have access to internet.

Social networks such as Facebook, MySpace, LinkedIn, Google groups, and Xing have become household brands in short span of time. This is one fascinating feature of internet: Everything happens so fast! Hence some of these internet business disappear equally rapidly. Nevertheless, almost one billion of the world population have a Facebook (fb) account today. About half of European internet users are also on fb, which means nearly 30 % fb penetration rate and it is over 50 % for North America. The implication for consumer behaviour is that through these variety of means, individuals around the world are connected and share information. They share what they like and what they do not like; they mobilise campaigns, petitions, even boycotts.

Segmentation and targeting with the help of fb and other social networks has been evolving in response to developments of the internet and increased connectivity. About 5 years ago, it was possible to argue that fb users are "smart, affluent, and internet-savvy people" (Holzner 2009) but today, as majority of people becoming part of it, there is no longer such easy associations. However, as the Founder and CEO of fb, Zuckerberg, correctly said in an interview in 2007 "nothing influences a person more than a recommendation from a trusted friend" (Story 2007). Within the contemporary transnational marketing and transnational

---

[4] See http://www.itu.int/ITU-D/ict/publications/yb/index.html.

consumers context, where this "trusted friend" is located does not really matter as much as it did in the past. Hence a new term, *e-geography* comes into play.

E-geography or electronic geography can be an extension to what Batty (1997, pp. 337–338) called "virtual geography" which he believes has risen as a result of "the emergence of virtual worlds which have their own sense of place and space, their own geography". The beauty and challenge of this virtual geography is that it does not necessarily resemble the real geographies of the world, countries, cities, and towns. Our transnationals can surf through, search, meet up with each other in the comfort of e-geography without the hassle of a physical move. It is cross-cutting market spaces, social spaces and personal spaces through the infinite number of connections between the nodes each of which represents something; a person, an organisation, a thing, product, a service, a place, anything else one can imagine.

Transnational consumers (including transnational mobiles) are part of these virtual communities and geographies. The online technology offers many advantages in terms of data availability and thus more precise targeting. However, many would argue that the basics of marketing have not been changed, particularly segmentation. Demographic variables are still very important for market segmentation. For example, Linkedin users are expected to be professionals who aim to maintain a network of trustworthy friends and business partners (Papacharissi 2009; Skeels and Grudin 2009). On the other hand fb tends to be dominated by a younger demographic where two-thirds are expected to be younger than 34 who are more interested in sharing fun stuff and personal experiences among friends and family.

This segment of (non-mobile) transnationals can therefore be further segmented by using psychographic and demographic variables to set up appropriate targeting strategies. For example, gender differences and diverse attitudes of different age groups are likely to moderate online behaviour whereas education and family outlook can have significant effect on the individuals' involvement with transnational networks. Again for instance, non-movers (or those who stay behind) who are part of households with one or more members living abroad or had experience of migration in the past are more likely to develop wider transnational connections compared to others. Migrants and mobile professionals, as well as transnational families (where members of the family are scattered in two or more countries), would be expected to have strong cross-border networks (see Penaloza 1995). Similarly, residents of global cities such as London are likely to develop rich transnational networks involving people from a variety of countries and cultural backgrounds (see Beaverstock and Smith 1996; Sassen 2002). One should also remember growing numbers of mixed-race individuals who often maintain some degree of connection to the countries from where their parents and grandparents are originally from. They also tend to be bilingual or multilingual. Hence all these consumers (e.g. dwellers of global cities and mixed race individuals) can be considered as members of an e-geography that may or may not correspond to physical boundaries of any nation state.

2.1 Connectedness and the Consumer E-Geography

The "transnational imagined communities" concept proposed by Cayla and Eckhardt (2008) helps to understand these borderless yet non-mobile consumers and how their identities are influenced and shaped by brands. Cayla and Eckhardt (2008) studied the role of brands in the creation of such transnational identities and connections, with a focus on Asian brands. Here the connectedness is built by consumption patterns and perceptions imposed by brands and marketing crossing the national boundaries. They explore within the regionalisation debate, how Asian companies moved from national association to regional association benefiting from increasing regional exchanges between Asian nations through online and print media while questioning the role of marketers in the process. These exchanges and connectedness contribute to the process of creating a sense of belonging and shared consciousness in the Asian region. Hence it is possible to talk about an emerging transnational Asian imagined community of consumers. This line of thinking is applicable to other parts of the world too; such as Latin America, Middle East, or Mediterranean.

This connectedness can possibly be treated in a rather conventional market segmentation. Online and wireless electronic connectedness is similar to roads and transport routes connecting locations without the limitations of physical move. Louvieris and Driver (2001) argued that the "marketing success in cyberspace depends on understanding IP address in the same sense that marketers can interpret postcodes or zip codes" (Sirkeci and Mannix 2010, p. 101). The fixed IP address would help to pin down consumers' lifestyle and behavioural choices within a geo-demographic segmentation model: Possible cyber-demographics use in market segmentation? Existing dynamic IP address models, and household noise would make such identification extremely difficult at individual level (Sirkeci and Mannix 2010). However, the level, intensity, type, and nature of connectivity (e.g. heavy users versus occasional users) can still be useful segmentation variables to understand and target these highly connected people.

2.2 Introducing Mobility and Movement as Segmentation Variables

In an earlier work, it was argued that for marketers, there is need for awareness of "human movement and mobility" which need to be included in our set of segmentation variables (Sirkeci and Mannix 2010, p. 95). The urge to conceptualise mobile consumers arises from a shift in consumer landscape, where borders are increasingly blurred. Movement of goods, services, finances, and finally of people have intensified in response to advances in transportation, communication and technology as well as increasing global integration through regional and global treaties (e.g. EU, NAFTA).

The key feature in this shift is increasing mobility and connectedness for people. For example, some of the very experienced consumers are benefiting from good pensions and savings and therefore they are very active and mobile. They often travel domestically and internationally and as a result spend considerable time away from their permanent, or usual, addresses. These older consumers also sometimes have families living in several locations (cities, towns and countries). Thus a considerable number among this so-called "Golden Age" segment is mobile. The changes in international secondary and higher education in certain regions, such as the European Union, facilitated the emergence of a large transnationally mobile student segment. Student exchange programmes carry students from country to country and exchange students spend substantial periods abroad through programmes such as Erasmus in Europe. Another example is transnationally mobile professionals. These work for large multinational corporations and sometimes by the nature of tasks, sometimes by company rules, they have to move between different countries or make regular trips to carry out tasks in different countries.

2.3 Early Scholarship on Mobiles

Consumer mobility is not a new phenomenon and yet consumers are more mobile today than, for example, 50 years ago. As mentioned above, many people spend substantial periods abroad. Among them are business people, holiday makers, students, immigrants, and staff of national and supranational organisations and governments. For instance, members of the European Parliament have to move between Brussels and Strasbourg almost on a weekly basis. This two-seat arrangement means these members of the European Parliament (MEPs) are practically working in two countries and possibly living in three countries making them a truly transnational group. The distinguishing feature of these consumer groups, compared to the resident or non-mobile populations, is 'movement' in their routines.

Marketers need to pay attention to the ways in which this mobility and movement feature can be taken on board in marketing planning. It leads us to the issue of integrating mobility as a variable in market segmentation. Our current segmentation toolbox includes some geographic and demographic variables. Thus it should be relatively easy to add new spatial variables. 'Place' as a variable is already well-established in marketing. Hence it is a key component in marketing mix considerations. Nevertheless, understanding and use of "place" in marketing analysis and planning are not refined enough to consider human mobility yet. Various available data sources such as censuses, labour force surveys and expenditure surveys include information on place of residence, commuting distance, birth place, change of residence, and sometimes directly on migration status. Thus, there is no reason for not developing marketing analysis and plans using the available information.

However, there has been little attempt to integrate movement into our understanding of market segments. Bell (1969) investigated the consumption patterns among households who changed their place of residence in the US. He named

2.3 Early Scholarship on Mobiles

them as *national mobiles* and *mobiles* in short. However, he was not specifically interested in the 'movement' variable. Bell conducted his study just a year after Andreasen (1966), who focused on conceptualisation of geographical mobility (i.e. change in residence) into market segmentation. In this pioneering study of mobility in marketing, he presented a strong case to show that a consumer segment, which he called *geographic mobiles,* are likely to have high purchasing power and likely to switch products, brands and stores (Andreasen 1966, p. 341). Surprising for him was the fact that while geographic location is sometimes the most important determinant of consumer attitudes and behaviour, change of geographic location was neglected.

Both Andreasen (1966) and Bell (1969) show us that 'national mobiles' who migrate between the US states are a large and lucrative segment worth targeting. These 'mobiles' are often relatively young (18–35), including disproportionately high number of ethnic minority members.

Marketing scholarship has not yet acknowledged movement as a segmentation variable though there is a growing literature on immigrant consumers for example. These focused on migrants' consumption patterns (Askegaard et al. 2005; Chung 2000), marketing of public transport (Frumkin-Rosengaus 1987), and immigrant minority consumers (Burton 2002). Not much change since Bell had underlined this fact by stating that "geographic location or residence has long been a recognised factor" but "change in residence has received very little attention" despite the fact that about 20 % of "American consumers change addresses each year" (1969, p. 37).

Bell's "mobiles" or "inter-county mobile families" were corresponding to three segmentation questions: Can we define a set of common lifestyle characteristics for these? Are their shopping behaviour is affected by being "mobile"? Can we reach them via standard marketing programmes or do we need to develop special ones? Then these mobiles were found to be relatively better off economically and socially and hence providing a lucrative opportunity for small or large businesses (Bell 1969, pp. 43–44). These consumers were rebuilding their consumption patterns in the new locations, destinations. Internal mobility levels are similarly large across the world. For example, in the UK, during the year ending June 2011, there were 2.59 million domestic moves reported, representing nearly 5 % of the total population (ONS 2012).[5]

Nevertheless, over a decades later, Albaum and Hawkins (1983, p. 97) were still trying to convince audiences that geographic mobility is an important variable as about 20 % of the US population was moving home every year. Gottko and Sauer (1989) revisited the issue to see if geographic mobility is relevant as a segmentation base. These studies revealed that mobile consumers represent a reasonably large segment and their demand and behaviour regarding particular products and services are likely to be different than non-movers. It was also noted that there were differences between long and short distance movers. This corresponds to our

---

[5] A significant portion of these are expected to be university students who change residence to go to university as the highest level of migration is reported for those aged 19.

Fig. 2.1 Mobility and mobile consumer segments

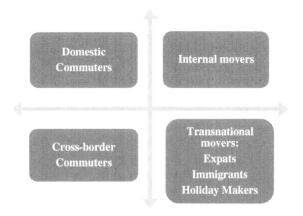

classification proposed in Fig. 2.1, where, along with the distance covered in movement, border crossing is added as a new dimension which allows us to identify 'transnational mobiles'. To represent different mobile consumer typologies, the axis x in Fig. 2.1 shows the distance of travel, movement whilst axis y indicating whether the individual crosses a national border or not.

National and transnational alike, mobile populations pose new challenges for marketers. On the one hand, they are likely to demand, for example, certain mobile services more than non-movers. Commuters, and distances to commute to work, become more relevant here. It is difficult to estimate the exact size of such commuting populations in global cities but one can comfortably say it is large. For example, it is estimated that the day-time population in City of London is about 30 times larger than the night time population. Such global cities also attract a good deal of transnational commuters who may stay a little longer e.g. few days.

Marketers need to take into account the fact that mobility itself is an important characteristic which may change consumer behaviour and trigger different needs, wants and desires. Moreover, mobility is likely to cause a substantial change in terms of consumers' cultural reference points. This means individuals would carry choices, preferences, tastes acquired in their places of origin, on the journey, and at the places of destination. Marketers categorising these mobile individuals need to consider these potential influences. A second generation Turkish individual from Berlin, Germany is likely to show different attitudes as a consumer compared to a Turk from Istanbul who never left Turkey. Similarly a Yorkshire man-became-Londoner would have London and Yorkshire in his set of cultural reference points compared to somebody who never travelled outside Yorkshire. The reference points are also important for decision making models. Consumer decision making, for example, regarding the value of a service or product, would be moderated by the fact that whether they have a single reference point or multiple reference points.[6]

---

[6] For a review of single and multiple reference points in decision making models, see Koop and Johnson (2012).

Now we have established that there is significantly large population segments who are ever more mobile within and beyond national boundaries. National mobiles, then, are comprised of long-distance and short-distance commuters and those who have moved between places. It must be also noted that these internal moves may mean drastic differences in cultural, social, economic and political environments in countries with larger geographies and multi-ethnic structures such as China and India. For example, a move from Kashgar in western China to Shanghai covers a vast physical distance (over 3,000 miles) as well as a significant cultural (Islam to Budhism) and socio-economic (small city to global industrial hub) distance. Then next step is to define and explore these transnational mobiles and any subgroups amongst them. Then it is possible to elaborate on the segment characteristics and attractiveness of such transnationals.

References

Albaum, G., & Hawkins, D. I. (1983). Geographic mobility and demographic and socioeconomic market segmentation. *Journal of the Academy of Marketing Science, 11*(1–2), 97–113.

Andreasen, A. R. (1966). Geographic mobility and market segmentation. *Journal of Marketing Research, 3*(4), 341–348.

Askegaard, S., Arnould, E. J., & Kjeldgaard, D. (2005). Postassimilationist ethnic consumer research: Qualifications and extensions. *Journal of Consumer Research, 32*(1), 160–170.

Batty, M. (1997). Virtual geography. *Futures, 29*(4/5), 337–352.

Beaverstock, J. V., & Smith, J. (1996). Lending jobs to global cities: Skilled international labour migration, investment banking and the city of London. *Urban Studies, 33*(8), 1377–1394.

Bell, J. E. (1969). Mobiles—A neglected market segment. *Journal of Marketing, 33*(2), 37–44.

Burton, D. (2002). Incorporating ethnicity into marketing intelligence and planning. *Marketing Intelligence and Planning, 20*(7), 442–451.

Cayla, J., & Eckhardt, G. M. (2008). Asian brands and the shaping of a transnational imagined community. *Journal of Consumer Research, 35*(2), 216–230.

Chung, E. (2000). Navigating the primordial soup: Charting the lived worlds of the migrant consumer. *Journal of Consumer Marketing, 17*(1), 36–54.

Cleveland, M., & Laroche, M. (2007). Acculturation to the global consumer culture: Scale development and research paradigm. *Journal of Business Research, 60*(3), 249–259.

Culley, L., & Hudson, N. (2010). Fertility tourists or global consumers? A sociological agenda for exploring cross-border reproductive travel. *International Journal of Interdisciplinary Social Sciences, 4*(10), 139–150.

Derne, S. (2008). *Globalization on the ground: New media and the transformation of culture, class, and gender in India*. London: Sage.

Figueiredo, B., & Cayla, J. (2012). *The transnational mobility of global cosmopolitans: How multi-acculturation affects the national identities of circulating consumers*. Paper presented at *European Marketing Academy Conference* (EMAC), Lisbon, Portugal.

Firat, A. F. (1997). Globalization of fragmentation: A framework for understanding contemporary global markets. *Journal of International Marketing, 5*(2), 77–86.

Frumkin-Rosengaus, M. (1987). *Increasing transit ridership through a targeted transit marketing approach*. Unpublished PhD thesis, State University of New Jersey, New Brunswick, NJ, USA.

Gottko, J., & Sauer, P. (1989). Household geographic mobility and the impact on macro market segments. Advances in consumer research proceedings. In T. K. Srull (Ed.), *Provo, UT: Association for consumer research*, Vol. 16, pp. 85–92.

Hannerz, U. (1992). *Cultural complexity: Studies in the social organization of meaning*. New York: Columbia University Press.

Holt, D. B., Quelch, J. A., & Taylor, E. L. (2004). How global brands compete. *Harvard Business Review, 82*(9), 68–75.

Holzner, S. (2009). *Facebook marketing: Leverage social media to grow your business*. Indiana: Que Pub.

Konrad, G. (1984). *Antipolitics*. New York: Harcourt Brace Jovanovich.

Koop, G. J., & Johnson, J. G. (2012). The use of multiple reference points in risky decision making. *Journal of Behavioral Decision Making, 25*, 49–62.

Levitt, T. (1983). The globalisation of markets. *Harvard Business Review, 61*(3), 92–102.

Louvieris, P., & Driver, J. (2001). New frontiers in cybersegmentation: marketing success in cyberspace depends on IP address. *Qualitative Market Research: An International Journal, 4*(3), 169–181.

ONS (Office for National Statistics). (2012). *Internal migration by local authorities in England and Wales, year ending June 2011*. Statistical Bulletin, Retrieved Sept 25, 2012 from http://www.ons.gov.uk/ons/dcp171778_280054.pdf.

Papacharissi, Z. (2009). The virtual geographies of social networks: a comparative analysis of Facebook, LinkedIn and ASmallWorld. *New Media & Society, 11*(1–2), 199–220.

Peñaloza, L. (1995). Immigrant consumers: Marketing and public policy considerations in the global economy. *Journal of Public Policy & Marketing, 14*(1), 83–94.

Sassen, S. (2002). Global cities and diasporic networks: Microsites in global civil society. In Marlies Galsius, Mary Kaldor, & Helmut K. Anheier (Eds.), *Global civil society* (pp. 217–238). Oxford: Oxford University Press.

Singh, N., Fassott, G., Chao, M. C., & Hoffmann, J. A. (2006). Understanding international web site usage: A cross-national study of German, Brazilian, and Taiwanese online consumers. *International Marketing Review, 23*(1), 83–97.

Sirkeci, I., & Mannix, R. (2009). *Transnational mobiles: A growing consumer segment.* Paper presented at the *Second International Conference on Social Sciences*, Social Sciences Research Society, Retrieved Sept 10–11, 2009, Izmir, Turkey.

Sirkeci, I., & Mannix, R. (2010). Segmentation challenges posed by 'transnationals' in mobile marketing. In Key Pousttchi & Dietmar G. Wiedemann (Eds.), *The handbook of research on mobile marketing management* (pp. 94–114). Hershey: IGI Global.

Skeels, M. M., & Grudin, J. (2009, May). When social networks cross boundaries: A case study of workplace use of facebook and linkedin. In *Proceedings of the ACM 2009 international conference on Supporting group work* (pp. 95–104). ACM.

Story, L. (2007) Facebook is marketing your brand preferences (with your permission). *The New York Times*. 7 November.

van der Pijl, K. (1998). *Transnational classes and international relations*. London: Routledge.

Chapter 3
Mobility and the Transnationals

In a recent conference paper by Figueiredo and Cayla (2012), mobile professionals who constantly move through different national cultures were called "circulating consumers". I suggest to frame these "circulating consumers" within our wider category of *mobile consumers* where movement and mobility is appropriately taken into account as key segmentation variables to identify these "mobile consumer groups" as shown in Fig. 2.1. The vertical axis in Fig. 2.1 shows domestic or cross-border character of the mobility while the horizontal axis shows the distance and duration of mobility. Hence we can distinguish commuters from movers (i.e. migrants) and internal movers and commuters from cross-border movers and commuters. Hence these latter ones should be called transnational mobiles.

The sub-segment of mobile consumers, "transnationally mobile consumers" can also be labelled in short as "transnationals". They are likely to switch between national allegiances and experience an overall weakening of allegiances to a single nation state or national cultural context and be inclined to have multiple cultural reference points. There we observe a multiplication of national allegiances among these consumers. Their mobility reaches beyond a single move from point A to point B or from country A to country B and this mobility triggers and contributes to a very dynamic multi-acculturation process.

The key is weakening ties among consumers to a single location as many study abroad, work abroad, and holiday abroad. However, there is a great variety within these mobile groups beyond the two axes, of distance and border crossing, drawn above. Segmentation of this group is therefore a demanding task. One way around is to focus on categories of mobility in terms of causes, motivations, and intentions. Thus, settlers, temporary migrants, high skilled migrants, students, and refugees can be classified as subgroups. However, other demographic categories based on gender, income, race and so on would cross cut these subgroups based on causes of mobility.

The difference between Bell's (1969) "national mobiles" and the transnationals is the border crossing or mobility beyond national borders. These are often both employees and customers of borderless/stateless companies. It is important to note here though we are not only thinking of migrants who often move from one place to another with a vision to settle for a long or limited period. Human mobility is a

I. Sirkeci, *Transnational Marketing and Transnational Consumers*,
SpringerBriefs in Business, DOI: 10.1007/978-3-642-36775-5_3,
© The Author(s) 2013

term that covers both those aiming to settle and those others who constantly move back and forth and across national borders where movement is in their routines of life.

With the exception of larger countries mentioned above, Bell's mobile nationals are likely to move shorter distances compared to the transnational mobiles. As we discussed elsewhere, transnationals crossing national borders often face a new set of rules, regulations, laws and new political environments. They move between different economic settings, cultural settings shaped up by different belief systems and attitudes. In certain cases, they move into a different technological environment too.

Transnational mobile consumers, at least some of them, are frequently moving between places and countries. This has not received much attention in the literature. However, significant number of works have been carried out on acculturation processes ethnic minorities and immigrant consumers are believed to go through. This literature followed the debates in Sociology and Anthropology from a distance as is often the case for business disciplines (Burton 2005). Thus, it was believed that these consumers with different backgrounds, that is different cultural reference points, would eventually assimilate into the mainstream consumer society as their tastes, preferences, and needs would converge over time. Askegaard et al. (2005, p. 160) find that among Greenlandic immigrants in Denmark "a transnational consumer culture emerges as an acculturative agent" as an unexpected outcome for post-assimilationist viewpoint. Later Üstüner and Holt (2007) found that hegemonic relationships shape the ways in which consumer acculturation develops; hence pointing out complexity of the process. The literature on identity is well developed Human Geography, Anthropology, and Sociology; identity is often multiple, relational, and changing, thus making understanding the acculturation process even more complex and difficult.

Nevertheless, the real question to be asked perhaps is nothing to do with acculturation or assimilation. Human mobility simply expands the networks individuals are involved with, exposes them to new relations and contexts, and in some cases this happens many times. This process may lead to an increased awareness as well as triggering the process of refining, redefining, and repositioning of oneself against the others, in relation to the others and in relation to one's own experiences all embedded in the context(s) individuals are leaving behind, passing through, stopping by, or arriving in. The transnational social space is simply multiplying the processes and offering a space of enactment for new identities. Therefore, although we can understand the multi-acculturation arguments (Figueiredo and Cayla 2012 and Askegaard et al. 2005), this transnational mobility process may not necessarily result in any acculturation but creates new (transnational) identities. Thus one can speak of the creation of transnational consumer cultures appropriate to the transnational "consumption-scapes".[1] Yet, these mobile individuals are likely to be aware of and responsive to new socio-

---

[1] Ger and Belk (1996) used the term "consumption scape" in another context.

cultural environments they are entering. The legal and customary codes about certain services and products such as tobacco, alcohol in these new environments are to be considered by these transnationals and thus their consumption behaviour is adjusted to the new environments.

Transnational mobility, on the other hand, is financially costly. Along with financial costs, it also requires a certain level of human capital and social capital to facilitate border crossing and life in another country.[2] This may mean being skilled, knowing other languages, having friends, acquaintances, and family abroad as well as good enough finances to cover the expenses of preparation and travel (e.g. visas, permits, travel, accommodation, etc.). Hence it is possible to argue that, at least a certain group, of transnationals are better off and likely to have higher incomes and/or wealthier than the ordinary consumer. No wonder this profile shall make transnationals more appealing to many businesses. Then the size matters. We have already looked at national mobiles who represent about 20 % in the US and nearly 5 % in the United Kingdom (UK) as mentioned earlier.

3.1 Mobile Population is Larger Than Migrant Population

Despite being one of the dominant topics in mainstream media and politics in many countries, particularly in the industrialised world, only about 3 % of the total world population reside outside their countries of birth. International Organisation for Migration (IOM) reports it to be around 214 million (www.iom.int). Mobility is not evenly spread around the world as some parts of the world witness more migration than others. For example in Europe and North America, about 9 and 13 % are overseas born respectively whilst this figure is 15 % for Oceania (UNDP 2008). Emerging markets and fast developing countries such as Brazil, Turkey, Russia are increasingly receiving more migrants but overall the share of immigrants in total population is relatively smaller in Asia, Africa, and Latin America. These statistics largely exclude the short term moves as official statistics are commonly compiled according to a United Nations definition of migration which is changing permanent place of residence for 12 months or more. Many of those professionals who frequently move between countries and yet stay lengthy periods but not enough to qualify for migrant status are often invisible in these statistics.

Therefore, travel statistics often indicate much larger figures. For instance, in the UK, reported total number of person trips for 2005 was nearly 95 million (ONS 2006). For 2011, UK Civil Aviation Authority (CAA) reported that almost 220 million went through the gates of UK airports while over 133 million were destined to London's five major airports. Obviously these figures include multiple trips by individuals and do not necessarily indicate such a huge migrating population but surely it is an indication of mass mobility. It simply indicates that there

---

[2] See Cohen et al. (2009) and O'Leary (2009).

Fig. 3.1 UK international travel and expenditures, 1980–2011. *Source* ONS (2012b)

is a movement carrying a population over three times larger than the country's official population size.

The UK travel statistics from 1980 to 2011 provide evidence for increased cross border travels, that is increased human mobility, and increasing spending by these mobile people (ONS 2012b). Figure 3.1 shows that the number of UK residents' visits abroad rose from 17.5 million in 1980 to 56.8 million by the end of 2011. The number of overseas visits to the UK nearly tripled to 30.8 million in the same period. The total spend by these international visitors (both directions) grew almost ten-fold, from a mere £5.6 billion to almost £50 billion in three decades. Again, among the British reported in this data set, there are people who make multiple visits every year. There are also others who never travel anywhere. However, yet, these figures are for a country with a population of just 63.2 million (ONS 2012a).

Similar statistics can be found for all other countries and global cities to underline the ever-increasing transnational mobility as well as transnational expenditure. For example in the US, total number of visitors went from 41.2 million in 2003 up to 62.3 million by the end of 2011.[3] In the same period the number of US citizens visiting other countries slightly increased from around 55 million to 60 million. In the meantime, historic figures on spending by visitors, inbound and outbound, indicates a steady increase: Americans' expenditure rose from around $2 billion in 1960 to around $14 billion in 1980, then to $48 billion in 1990, to $89 billion in 2000, and finally $110 billion in 2011. Since the end of 1980s, the US began receiving more tourism revenues than what her own citizens spend abroad. Spending by visitors to the US rose from about $1 billion in 1960, to over $13 billion in 1980 and to $153 billion in 2011. Although US is one of the largest markets in the world, these two figures put together represent a total volume ($263 billion) which is larger than most countries GDP (USDoC 2012). According to the World Tourism Organisation Statistics, the number of

---

[3] Following the New York attacks there was a sharp decline in visitor numbers in 2001 and 2002.

3.1 Mobile Population is Larger Than Migrant Population 39

international tourists who stayed overnight almost doubled from 535 million in 1995 to 1,035 million in 2012, over half of whom were reported in Europe.[4] Usually about a quarter of these visits are for business purposes indicating a significant market for needs other than leisure.

3.2 Sub-groups Within Transnational Mobiles

The fact appears to be that transnational mobiles making over a billion trips every year may represent a gigantic market. However, within this large population, there is a great diversity. They surely share some common characteristics but we will first look into potential sub-segments which may present more precise and attractive marketing opportunities.

Transnational mobiles are both consumers and providers; they are marketers too. They do move around the world and consume products and services satisfying their distinct needs arising from the fact of being mobile. Among them are tourists, business people, entrepreneurs, highly skilled professionals, and various kinds of immigrants e.g. working holiday makers, students, refugees, seasonal workers, and the like.[5] Their needs and wants, thus consumption and expenditure patterns, can be relatively different from their fellow citizens left behind in the origin country and those in their destination(s) (i.e. non-movers, non-mobiles). Holiday makers and professionals working in multiple or far away locations should also be considered in this category, which we term as 'transnationals' because of their links, networks and complex reference points reaching beyond any single national context. These people establish links with their friends, families, partners in diasporas (e.g. Indian diaspora, Jewish diaspora, Turks in Europe) as well as those in their countries of origin. They foster new cultures and experiences while the cultural baggage they carry remain to be of interest to marketers.

Then the important question for marketers is how these customers will be identified and segmented? What will be the reference points that we need to take into account contextual characteristics while setting up marketing plans targeting these mobile people? Is it their country of origin or the destination matters more?

The transnational mobiles can be categorised under two main groups: Migrants and non-migrants, based on the criteria of changing place of residence for 12 months or more as the UN definition suggests. Figure 3.2 illustrates the sub-groups within these two broader categories. The ones within the red circle are core migrant groups whereas others do not always comply with the 12 month criteria. Nevertheless some groups may also include people who falls within the migrant

---

[4] Available from http://www.unwto.org.

[5] "Transnational entrepreneurs" are an interesting group, for example. They are defined as entrepreneurs who undertake cross-border business activities (see Özden and Schiff 2005). These are considered in relation to 'brain drain' and 'brain circulation' and even called astronauts as they spend substantial amount of time on airplanes (Saxenian 2002 and 2006, p. 318).

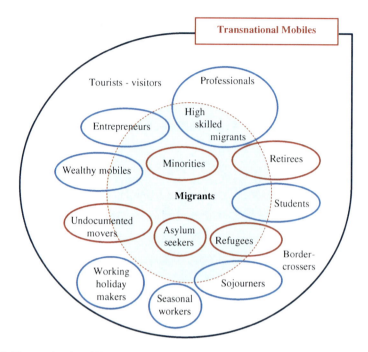

Fig. 3.2 Transnational mobile segments

category and these are shown overlapping in the Fig. 3.2. Some of these categories are more mobile than others. For example, professionals, entrepreneurs, and sojourners are frequent travellers whereas asylum seekers, refugees and undocumented movers are less mobile due to their unique legal circumstances which often impose limitations on their movement within and between countries.

3.2.1 Transnational Professionals and High Skilled Migrants

One of the leading consultancy firms argue that globally minded leaders are needed to advance projects and it takes a "borderless approach to recruiting top talent". This particular firm employs about a quarter of a million professionals and receives over 1.6 million job applications from around the world. Mobile professionals attracted some attention from companies who are providing mobile services particularly in the communications sector.[6] Mobile professionals can be

---

[6] It seems most focus is on white collar office professionals but one should remember that there are other professionals such as plumbers, mechanics, medical staff who are very mobile too, although these are unlikely to be transnationally mobile.

employed by transnational companies or organisations as well as other firms with international operations and links. Company executives, specialist consultants such as information technology (IT) consultants, engineers, ministers of religion, professors teaching in transnational campuses, university officers involved in overseas operations fall into this group. This group includes a good number of high income managers. For example, in a comparative study, 38 % of executive directors of the top 100 firms in France and 48 % in the UK were "foreign" while the share among non-executive directors were 64 and 62 % respectively (Harvey and Maclean 2010, p. 119). Intra-company transfers is also part of this broad segment of transnational mobile professionals.

> *Acculturation process poses interesting challenges for multinational companies with significant numbers of expat managers. These do go through a multi-acculturation process as they move between countries and some studies argued that the failure in acculturation costs companies in excess of $50,000 per manager along with some difficult-to-measure costs such as decline in self-esteem* (Mendenhall and Oddou 1985, p. 39). *Nevertheless, the acculturation process is facilitated by the flow of finances, goods, information, ideas, and people to create individuals who are influenced and shaped by multiple cultures* (Craig and Douglas 2006).

Intra-company transfers represent a unique and privileged category among transnational mobiles. They are often not subject to the usual immigration controls. They represent about two-thirds of those registered in high skilled migrant programmes. Their admissions are often treated preferentially for a few reasons: First, they are transferred on a temporary basis—e.g. in the UK, these can stay up to 5 years. As a manager of a pharmaceutical firm suggested, this assignments are lengthy for a reason: "If you are trying to form a relationship with a government as a country manager, you are not going to do that in three years. Four years is still a bit short... probably five years" (Salt and Wood 2013, p. 99). Secondly they are either at managerial or executive levels or in possession of specialist knowledge and skills which are considered to be in shortage and uncommon in general labour market.

Supranational and regional organisations such as the European Union, the United Nations, and the UNICEF also mobilise their members of staff transnationally. For instance the members of the European Parliament have to commute between their constituencies and the Parliament sessions held in Brussels and Strasbourg. Similarly, workers of UNHCR, the UN agency dealing with refugees around the world have to spent substantial periods abroad in the field while some others visit multiple sites on a regular basis. Similarly, professors employed for transnational education programmes of universities (e.g. Nottingham, UK, Middlesex, UK, Yale, US, Webster, US) may be required to spend lengthy periods away in their campuses in Dubai, Malaysia, or China.

These professionals live abroad for relatively varying periods from a few days or weeks to 6 months or more. They often work on specific projects or meet with their clients, providing training, consultancy and giving lectures. Many of them are expected to travel alone or with colleagues while some also take their families along. In fact many of them might be single.

This professional mobile group is believed to be significantly large among transnational mobiles and their mobility is increasing (Beaverstock and Faulconbridge 2010). The total number of business travel miles increased about one-third in the 2000s (Faulconbridge and Beaverstock 2008). Similar to other countries in Western Europe, business travel has grown rapidly in the UK (ONS 2006 and 2012b). While international travel for business purposes have doubled in the last two decades, average length of stay for business trips is around 5 nights. In fact, travels between the UK, France, and Germany constitute about 25 % of total number of visits to and from the UK whilst travels from and to Europe represent about 75 % of this market in the UK travel industry.

There are motives for corporations to source within their internal labour markets and move staff around the world. Salt and Wood (2013) refer to categories such as commuter assignments of key experts who commute weekly over periods up to 2 years or "extended business travel" ranging from a month to six months. Some companies prefer to shift staff internationally when they set up new subsidiaries in another country until the local staff are trained and available (Salt and Wood 2013, p. 91). They quote a manager stating "We have to move these people around the world to where we have the global centres of that particular type of work" or the "business is based on a very specific knowledge, skills, research. So it requires a lot of movement of the very highly specialised, may be research scientists" (Salt and Wood 2013, pp. 98–99). In other cases, the need is drawn from the company's staff training policy and client requirements as one IT manager points out: "we actively rotate people back to India" to make sure the off-shore team get a real appreciation of the client needs (Salt and Wood 2013, p. 101).

For example, in a small higher education institution in central London, one can find a professor who lives in Germany and travels to London frequently to teach his classes on management. At the same institution, another lecturer based in Barcelona travels several times a year to teach a master class while another colleague travels from Turkey to teach his well demanded class each Spring semester. Each one of them spends a good deal on travel and accommodation as they often stay in London for periods ranging from a few days to a few weeks for each set of teaching.

Mobile professionals are required to deliver services in multiple locations. That may mean a heavy reliance on mobile services such as mobile phones, wireless internet, e-mail as well as resources and support which would be easily available in an office setting. When working, mobile professionals can also be required to work in unconventional environments such as in a car, in a café, hotel, station, or airport. These are features likely to incur higher costs when staff are on the move which goes beyond simple travel costs. For example business people who spend a substantial portion of their working week travelling, equipped with mobile services via laptops, mobile phones and other smart devices are called "Techno Road Warriors" (Schiffman et al. 2008, p. 52).

High skilled migrants are considered among transnational professionals because they share similar characteristics overall. However, their cross-border moves are often self-initiated and motivated by career prospects. They are not sent by companies but travel on their own initiative (Ariss and Syed 2011, p. 288). They are likely to be subjected to stricter border controls compared to intra-company transfers but still likely to be relatively more mobile and wealthier. As in many countries, when such admission systems in place, high income is imposed as eligibility criteria.[7] Medical doctors and IT specialists are such professionals and also they overlap with immigrants category. For example, overseas doctors constitute a significant share of those in the profession in many industrialised countries such as New Zealand, where more than a third of doctors are overseas (MOHnz 2008), and the UK, where around 25 % of consultants have overseas qualifications (Goldacre et al. 2004).

3.2.2 Transnational Entrepreneurs

Portes et al. (2002) present transnational entrepreneurship as an alternative way of immigrant adaptation as these individuals are believed to mobilise their cross country social networks to succeed economically. They benefit from a web of contacts created by immigrants and their home country counterparts who engage in a pattern of repeated back-and-forth movements across national borders in search of economic advantage and political voice (Portes et al. 2002). Transnational entrepreneurs are a significant group. For instance, Morawska (2004) names three types only in New York: "Chinese global traders", "Jamaican ethnic entrepreneurs", and "Dominican small-scale investors". Chinese global entrepreneurs are found even in tiny nations such as Cape Verde (Haugen and Carling 2005).

These entrepreneurs tend to move, even commute, between their countries of origin and host, taking care of their investments in both places. They very rarely move into third countries. According to a Canadian study, a typical transnational entrepreneur is a 45-year-old or older man who is married with one child, likely to have a Master's degree, with no full-time job and he moves to another country seeking business opportunities and, subsequently, looks for business expansion by drawing resources from dual locations (Lin and Tao 2012).

The survey of 1198 firms conducted in the US by Portes et al. (2002) reveal a consumption and business pattern spanning across home and host countries. Typical transnational entrepreneurs invest in their home countries while about one-third import goods from their home countries. About a quarter travels at least twice

---

[7] In the UK, earning requirement for eligibility in high skilled immigration category can be as high as £45,000 minimum (UKBA 2007).

a year and about sixth travels six times or more every year. Nevertheless, the key fact is that these individuals' consumption behaviour is shaped by distinct sets of environmental structures, including cultural repertoires, social and professional networks and power relations carried over and gained through travels (Terjesen and Elam 2009, p. 1105).

Dominicans in New York is an interesting case, because they are framed as "temporary" movers in the discourse of the Dominican government (Itzigsohn et al. 1999). Constantly moving between the two countries, these transnational mobiles invested substantially in the residential construction industry in the Dominican Republic. In response to this demand, Dominican construction and real estate firms became regular advertisers in the immigrant media in New York City while new development projects in Dominican Republic largely designed for, targeted and marketed to the expatriate community (i.e. transnational entrepreneurs) (see Portes et al. 2002). Hence we can identify here the influence of transnational mobiles on the marketing mix of a national construction industry.

These entrepreneurs typically forge ties between the sectors in their country of origin and destination on a daily basis. Kamber, the Turkish manager of a cultural association in Germany "have to deal with Turkey almost every day... work closely with ministries and cultural organisations in Turkey... deal with artists ... record companies" (Faist et al. 2013, p. 32). Their cultural ties, or cultural reference points determine their business behaviour as well as consumer behaviour. For example, another Turkish entrepreneur from Germany, Ozlem, aged fifty-five, selling evening and wedding dresses sources them from factories in Turkey. She goes to Turkey "for business for 10 days and stay for the weekend to see her daughter who runs a fashion store in Turkey" (Faist et al. 2013, p. 36).

3.2.3 Wealthy Mobiles

More affluent people are more able to travel as they wish. Around the world, most migration admission regimes favour such clients. Wealthy mobiles largely overlap with the tourist segment which can be segmented into income/wealth categories. Luxury mobiles fall under luxury consumers segment spending which has grown significantly even during the most recent global financial crisis. The total value of the global luxury segment is estimated to be above $140 billion dollars.

Defining the luxury consumer is open to debate and there is significant variety around the world. In the US, wealthy often represents a total household income of $500,000 and above. The size of the segment is difficult to assess. However, in China alone, there is estimated to be about 2.7 million US dollar millionaires. They tend to travel abroad more often. For example, the average number of trips among Chinese luxury travellers was 3.1 in 2012 for whom the main destinations were countries such as US, France, Maldives, UK, and Italy (Hurun 2012).

Typically these luxury consumers are internet savvy and interested in new technologies. Around three quarters of them are active users of Facebook. They like customised products and generally expect their expectation of products and services offered to be met or exceeded. Among the Chinese super rich, over 60 % reported travelling as their favourite leisure activity on which they spent close to one-third of their annual discretionary spending of $277,000 (Hurun 2012). This represents a very lucrative transnational mobile consumer segment.

3.2.4 Tourists and Visitors

Tourists and visitors are in many ways similar to wealthy mobiles but they are not as fortunate in terms of wealth. The variety in tourist types makes them suitable for multiple sub-segments using geo-demographic and psychographic/lifestyle variables. For example, there are tourists travelling in organised groups as well as others who make an effort to get off the beaten track. Then there are those who prefer comfort and central locations with touristic attractions as opposed to others who prefer to get as far away as possible from home and anything familiar to immerse into the culture of local people in destinations. These groups spending patterns differ along with their life styles, desires and wants. A further distinction can be made between those tourists who are visiting family or friends as their needs and wants as well as the ways in which these are addressed would vary.

Among tourists there are also groups with a mission. One such group is pilgrims who are on a journey to a holy place. For instance, every year, around three million Muslims visit Mecca for *Hajj* and *Umrah* and stay there up to 6 weeks. Thousands of Jewish pilgrims also travel to Jerusalem to pray at the Wailing Wall every year. Similarly thousands of Christians visit Jerusalem, Virgin Mary's House, and other holy sites mentioned in Bible, in a less structured fashion.

A more frequent traveller group is football fans who follow their teams around continents for glory. Leading football clubs, such as Barcelona FC, Manchester United, and Real Madrid have fan bases everywhere but their local supporters like any other team go to their matches in European Champions League and other tournaments. This may entail about a dozen away games every year and hence means a significant mobility for each fan base. The football fans also travel across the World for national teams playing at the World Cup. They can be considered as part of the temporarily mobile consumer segment. These football fans are similar to non-travelling fans, but they are likely to have a higher income and therefore would need a range of services and products that non travelling fans wouldn't.

Sitting in between tourists/visitors and immigrants, there are retirees or elderly consumers. Sudbury and Simcock (2009), for example, proposed two segments of the elderly, one of which is *Positive Pioneers* who constitute 30 % elderly the population in the UK (about 5.2 million). These are people in their mid-50s, relatively affluent, healthy, in frequent contact with their families, and they take most of their holidays abroad. Nevertheless, as mentioned above, the number of visitors around the world has been on the rise year on year during the recent decades and in 2012 the total visits per annum exceeded the 1 billion threshold.

3.2.5 Students

Increasingly more and more students are becoming mobile. The European Union promotes student and academic mobility across 28 member states in the Union. Internationalisation of the curriculum and transnational education have been important agenda items. For example the UK Higher Education Academy supports two special interest groups in these two not so unrelated fields. University rankings usually include some direct or indirect indicator on overseas students and praise institutions with higher proportion of international students. All these create an environmental impetus so universities forge more and more partnerships with universities in other countries. For example, Regent's College, a small private university in London claims to have about 150 partner institutions around the world.[8] Students who can move or benefit from existing mobility schemes typically spend periods ranging from 4 months to 4 years. However, even those staying longer periods tend to stay term times only and either travel or return home for holidays. Often they spend about 9 months in countries where they study. This is why many of students are not reported as migrants in census statistics.

In the UK, the number of overseas students enrolled in higher education has grown from around 300,000 in 2005 to over 435,000 in 2012 (HESA 2012; Sirkeci et al. 2010). Overall, the contribution of these students to economy is estimated to be in excess of £5 billion (Millar and Salt 2008).

Similar to the university students, there is a sizeable number of young researchers who are mobile professionals often on some sort of training scheme. These transnational research staff constitute between 24 to 59 % of the total number of research staff employed in the UK (Smetherham et al. 2008). Many of these individuals are at earlier stages of their professional careers and often working abroad to gain experience with little or no intention to settle.

Both transnational students and research staff are likely to live on limited budgets and therefore tend to live in shared accommodation. It has implications for consumption and marketing. For example, in these shared houses, individual tenants or lodgers likely to use mobile services (e.g. mobile phones and mobile internet) as these places unlikely to have multiple landlines. As a result, this is a prime target segment for mobile devices and mobile services.

3.2.6 Immigrants

When we talk about human mobility, immigrants are the first category to cross our minds. This is rightly so as they constitute the largest stable transnational segment. As mentioned earlier, settled or long-term (i.e. staying more than 12 months) immigrant population in the world is about 220 million strong. Profiles of

---

[8] http://www.regents.ac.uk/ipo.aspx.

immigrants may differ by countries of origin and destination. International demand for particular skills and qualifications as well as shortages determine the composition. Hence the challenges immigrants face and services and products they need differ.

For example, dominantly Muslim Gulf countries in the Middle East host a large number of foreign domestic carers as well as contractors. Both occupational categories combined with the societal and cultural traditions in these countries result in a significant segments of single male contract workers and female carers. Among both gender groups, there are parents who left their families behind in their countries of origin. Certain products and services would appeal to these segments, for example to maintain their long distance family relationships.

Immigrant consumers tend to use their mother tongue at home and are viewers of ethnic TV channels (Aksoy 2006). Other studies point that ethnic enclaves emerge and offer economic opportunities to immigrant minorities (see Portes and Shafer 2006; Zhou 2004; Sirkeci 2009; Khattab et al. 2010). Residential concentration of ethnic and immigrant minorities is an advantage for marketers when it comes to reaching these customers and targeting.

This segment is also preyed upon by fraudsters. NICE[9] in New York, in fact, supports a campaign run by Urban Justice Centre[10] against consumer frauds committed against immigrants by immigration attorneys and employment agencies that actively target immigrant segment (NICE and GDP 2012). Indeed, immigration services including legal aid, consultancy and public services such as visas, passports are an untapped field of research from a marketing perspective. Perhaps using Service-Dominant logic, the inner workings of marketing in this sector needs to be unravelled.

Investigating these consumption processes and patterns as well as marketing practices, there is a growing literature on immigrant consumers with a focus on a range of issues including acculturation, identity, assimilation and products, services and costs (e.g. Donthu and Cherian 1994; Lee and Tse 1994; Venkatesh 1995; Wang 2004; Webster 1994).

Many studies show that immigration is age and gender selective. Thus, younger individuals are dominant. This might be true for most but there is also the retirement migration phenomenon (e.g. Gustafson 2001; Illes 2005). These elderly transnational mobiles experience multiple place attachment and face cultural differences between home and retirement destinations while pursuing seasonal migrations between the two locations for stays typically ranging from a couple of months to 6 months. Among Swedish transnational elderly mobiles, Gustafson (2001) identifies three ideal–typical transnational lifestyles: *translocal normality*,

---

[9] New Immigrant Community Empowerment (NICE) is a community-based organization and worker center that helps new immigrants build social, political, and economic power in their communities and beyond (www.nynice.org).

[10] Community Development Project at the Urban Justice Centre supports grassroots organisations (www.cdp-ny.org).

multilocal adaptation and *routinised sojourning* reflecting different strategies for managing cultural differences and mobility patterns.

Alongside retirees targeting better climates and affordable areas in other countries, there are other *sojourners* and seasonal workers. Sojourners are those who move internationally but without aiming to settle. They do stay lengthy periods and may repeat the sojourn several times over life time. By 1980, nearly half of Mexican immigrants were estimated to be sojourners, which declined to around 28 % by 1990 and to about 16 % in the late 1990s (Cornelius and Marcelli 2000, pp. 8–9). These immigrants often aim at saving money as they would have a project to fund upon their return to home or have a timed need for extra income such as school fees, wedding expenses etc. It is in the definition: Sojourners are "those who, after accumulating a certain amount of money, would return to the country of origin" (Cornelius and Marcelli 2000, p. 15).

Seasonal workers however are a category created by the needs of certain sectors. These people often are employed in agriculture, tourism, and construction sectors. They move to countries with labour shortages during the peak seasons and return after. Since these are short-term moves, these individuals and/or families are likely to have stronger ties with those left behind and therefore their needs for mobile communication services can be higher. Unlike immigrants, they would not face much of acculturation pressure. Hence switching behaviour possibly can be triggered only because of unavailability of certain products and services the seasonal workers used to consume at home. This segment can also serve as carriers of products and brands between the seasonal work destination and the place of origin.

Due to the nature of work, these people tend to be mostly healthy and young men and women, depending on the sector. For example, there were about 1.75 million seasonal farm workers in the US (Martin 2013). National Centre for Farmworker Health Inc. in the US reports[11] the average age of seasonal migrant farm workers in the US is 36, more than three quarters of them are males, and majority are married with children. Only about 30 % can speak English well. Only about 5 % have health insurance. Thus, for instance, marketers can see here a Spanish speaking market opportunity for insurance products.

Working holiday makers (WHM) are also often fall into seasonal workers category. There is a need for seasonal workers in, for example, the tourism sector in many countries. For example, more than 185,000 working holiday makers visas[12] were issued in 2010/11 in Australia and average spending by these holiday makers was estimated to be over $13,500 (USD) during their stay which can be as long as 8 months (ATEC 2012). In just two decades, WHM numbers increased 6–7 times, indicating an exponential growth in this particular segment of transnational mobiles. Tan et al. (2009) describe these transnational mobiles, i.e. WHMs, as well educated, aged 20–30 years old, travel around for experience, typically stay for

---

[11] See http://www.ncfh.org/docs/fs-Migrant%20Demographics.pdf.

[12] These visas are issued to individuals aged up to 30–35 in Australia, New Zealand, and Canada.

8 months, mostly move around the destination country during their stay, and spend around $13,000.

Finally, there are also those who cross a national border on a daily basis or at least frequently. These are people living in borderlands such as Ukrainian and Polish border, Turkish and Iraqi border, Laos and Thailand border. Often these borders are drawn according to some political and administrative concerns and divide nations, ethnic groups, and families while also dividing once united market places. Nevertheless, trade does not necessarily stop. For instance, smuggling of goods through the mountainous borders between Iran, Iraq, and Turkey has been a known phenomenon for decades for example. Differences in prices and earnings on two sides of national borders also facilitates such cross-border activity.

However, what matters is the connectivity and maintained ties between places which result in continued exchanges and trips. For example, Emre was brought to Germany at age 8 by his *guestworker* parents and yet he usually flies to Turkey once a year while maintaining very good contacts with his relatives in Turkey (Faist et al. 2013, p. 29). Or it is a transnational mother in the US, who "is here, but there" taking care of her children in Mexico (Hondagneu and Avila 1997, p. 313).

Refugees and asylum seekers are a sub-category of immigrant segment. Relatively smaller in size than other migrant categories, they may not be as settled as others since we have cases where refugees are held as temporary visitors for decades or asylum seekers living in limbo for extended periods. Nevertheless, they do maintain their ties across borders and often maintain a transnational lifestyle where these connections with the country of origin and other Diaspora communities are vital. Legal statuses of these groups have an impact on their mobility, their income and thus consumption patterns. For example, some asylum seekers in certain countries are tied to a location or dispersed around the country with or without their consent. Also in most cases, they are not allowed to work which restricts their income and in return spending patterns are determined. "They often live in purpose built centres and/or are subject to close monitoring. This bars them choosing a 'normal' life style where they can get land lines, permanent addresses and have access to a range of communication services" (Sirkeci and Mannix 2010). Therefore, a special attention is needed to understand and target these consumers. As a temporal group, they would have closer ties with their countries of origin and as their uncertain resident status implies, there is a chance of immediate and sudden return to home (Gibney 2008).

Undocumented mobiles are another similarly temporal but distinct sub-category who are often named 'undocumented', 'illegal', or 'clandestine' movers. The size, location and characteristics of this segment is very difficult to assess. However, they are believed to be similar to immigrant groups, which implies similar in consumption patterns while being restricted in terms of mobility patterns and their access to official, legal services. Some of these are expected to be among other "documented" groups such as some seasonal farm workers are undocumented in in the US and Germany (Hess 2006). As an unidentifiable and hard to assess and hard to reach group, this may not be a lucrative group to target. However, the fluidity of undocumented and others is obvious. For example, those individuals whose visas expire become over-stayers, or undocumented. These are likely to be part of ethnic and immigrant enclaves and therefore locating them might be possible. Obviously among the undocumented, there will be a variety in terms of income and other characteristics. It is very likely many of these will be on low incomes. The sheer size of the undocumented group makes it appealing. Estimates often indicate that the undocumented population is larger than the number of registered immigrants in many countries. Nevertheless, one should always consider ethical and legal implications potentially involved in targeting this group.

> **Box 1. Minority consumers in the UK**
> Minority populations in the UK are significantly younger than the national average. Comprised of South Asians, Africans, Caribbeans, and others their share and geographical spread is increasing. Many of them, such as Indians, are multiple car owners whilst they live in larger households. They love to drive a BMW and spend a lot more on hair products as well as consuming 'ethnic' food.
> *Source*: IPA (2012)

Immigrant consumer segments to some extent overlap with minority consumer segments that were originally created as a result of immigration. Mr Debarshi Pandit, head of Omnicom Media Group Ethnic in the UK says "a good chunk of second-or-third generation ethnic minorities who are well integrated into British society, still want a link to their 'own' culture." Own culture here refers to their transnational ties to the country(ies) of origin. This particular segment is growing in many countries such as in the UK. These consumer transnational connectedness is likely to be higher than the native consumers. For example, an Ofcom (2003) survey showed that ethnic minority consumers perceive some brands to be disproportionately associated with country of origin and these (Asian) brands remained strong in the community.

Industry seems not fully targeting these ethnic minority consumers despite the significant size and relatively attractive potential market opportunities. There is a delicate balance to be maintained when there are tensions among and about ethnic and minority groups. Marriott hotels saw a strong boycotting campaign in 2008 and since then they are actively targeting these very groups. Although there are increasingly more and more channels at marketers' disposal (IPA 2012), it may not be that easy to segment and target the groups such as minorities, mobiles and transnationals. It is time to turn to successful segmentation strategies.

3.3 Segmentation for Transnationals and Mobiles

Marketers paid attention to ethnic minority consumers to tap into a lucrative market, estimated to be around £300 billion in the UK,[13] but mobility and movement are generally missing items in their tool boxes. To identify segments we need to look at how distinct these are from others while also seeking homogeneity among the members of the segment. However, there are also other concerns. Earlier studies (e.g. Bell 1969; Andreasen 1966; Quigley and Weinberg 1977) did not test the homogeneity but made suggestions about distinguishing long distance mobiles from short distances mobiles. Therefore spatial mobility as a segmentation base has not been tested. While Quigley and Weinberg (1977) suggesting intra-urban mobiles as a distinct segment, Dickson (1981) proved in a role-playing experiment that mobility status did not influence the choice between chain stores and local stores.

Wedel and Kamakura (2000, pp. 9–10) divide segmentations bases along the lines of being observable and unobservable, where segments derived from the observable bases are believed to be easier to communicate and implement. Segmentation is simply a process of classifying customers into groups. It became an essential element of marketing in industrialised countries since its introduction by Smith (1956) as a concept derived from the heterogeneity of customer wants that need to be satisfied more precisely. It is an essential part of the marketers tool box in effective marketing planning. With precise segmentation, the firm can come up with marketing strategies to build the right relationships with the right customers (Kotler and Keller 2008, p. 410). In today's increasingly borderless world, internet and wireless connection technologies are both complicating the process and offering opportunities. Changes in the market environment such as new developments in information technology and connectedness across borders provides marketers a much richer dataset about customers and provides direct access to customers networks. Hence conventional approaches to segmentation comes under question (Day and Montgomery 1999). Nevertheless, common segmentation variables remain useful and multinational companies are interested in segmenting markets that cut across geographic and administrative boundaries. These variables include demographic characteristics such as gender, age, education, occupation, income; geographic characteristics including place of residence, area characteristics; user and usage dependent categories of behaviour and mixtures.

Wedel and Kamakura (2000) offer a model (Table 3.1) where customers are broadly divided along the lines of observability and customer/product characteristics. General variables are independent of products, services and circumstances/ context as opposed to product specific variables which link both customers, products and the context and circumstances of consumption. Then the other axis is based on whether one can measure these variables directly (observable) or indirectly (unobservable). Among the general variables, marketers can identify segments such

---

[13] This seems an overestimation compared to what Sirkeci (2009) claims (i.e. £30 bn) but the point is to show that there is significant market.

Table 3.1 General and product specific segmentation variables. Adapted from Wedel and Kamakura (2000, p. 7)

	Observable	Unobservable
General	Cultural, geographic, demographic and socio -economic variables: e.g. mobile or not	Psychographics, values, personality and life-style: e.g. cosmopolitan
Product-specific	User status, usage frequency, store loyalty and patronage, situations: e.g. forced to switch due to unavailability of products/services	Psychographics, benefits, perceptions, elasticities, attributes, preferences, intention: e.g. tend to switch-less loyal

as upper middle class (i.e. demographic) or multi-racial areas or "*boomers and babies* (i.e. geo-demographic) who go jogging, have a mortgage, watch MTV, read Sunset [magazine] and are into personal computing" (Wedel and Kamakura 2000, p. 243). Rogers' (1962, cited in Wedel and Kamakura 2000, p. 10) classification based on stage of adoption is an example of product specific and observable variables. Psychographic segmentation would consider values, lifestyle choices and personality characteristics as well as consumer perceptions. For instance, *needs based segmentation*, where marketers group customers based on what they want to do, would fall under product-specific unobservable category (Greengrove 2002).

Marketers can consider an infinite number of combinations taking into account various features and factors within the four categories of variables (Table 3.1). Not all segments and everybody are potential customers and therefore strategic choices have to be made. Therefore, every organisation works on virtually unique segmentation framework. For instance, three quarters of the pharmaceutical companies in the UK segmented the market by end use, purchase volume, purchasing situations, and price sensitivity (Weinstein 2004, pp. 8–9). However, segmentation categories need to be evaluated against the successful segmentation criteria.

Successful segments should be measurable in size, purchasing power and other characteristics, large enough to be viable and profitable if targeted, easy to reach and distinguishable (Hill and O'Sullivan 2004, p. 165). Wind (1978) underlined the importance of homogeneity and the need for segmentation, that is whether it can be targeted as a whole. Taking on board Wind and others, Wedel and Kamakura (2000) proposed six criteria to assess segments. Accordingly, segments should be measurable and distinguishable from others (*identifiability*), *stable* over time, and large enough to generate profits (*substantiality*). Potential segments proposed within the transnational mobility framework are seemingly identifiable

3.3 Segmentation for Transnationals and Mobiles

Table 3.2 Active mobile broadband subscriptions per 100 inhabitants, 2011

Region	2011
Europe	54.10
The Americas	30.49
World	17.00
Commonwealth of Independent States (CIS)	14.93
Arab states	13.25
Asia and Pacific	10.74
Africa	3.79

Source (ITU 2007)

and stable (although this appears ironic with our focus on mobility and movement). Many of the sub segments such as wealthy mobiles or transnational professionals should be reasonably profitable. Access to mobile broadband across world regions are presented in Table 3.2. This is a service area of particular interest to transnational mobile consumers and it indirectly shows the proportion of individuals who might be in need of internet connection when on the move. Hence it is clear that there are substantial markets in Europe and North America where the access rates are as high as 54 %.

"*Accessibility* is the degree to which managers are able to reach the targeted segments through promotional and distributional efforts" which is closely linked to distributional challenge coverage (Wedel and Kamakura 2000, p. 4). For instance, the elderly segment of *Positive Pioneers* mentioned earlier can be accessed through magazines, the Internet, and television (Sudbury and Simcock 2009). Highly mobile business executives can be reached, for example, through publications targeting business class travellers.

Responsiveness means segments, which are homogeneous, must respond uniquely to marketing efforts targeted at them. For example Dubois et al. (2005) identified three segments in 20 countries in terms of consumers attitude towards luxury: Democratic, distance, and elitist. Each group span across national borders: for example, the democratic group is comprised of Danish, New Zealanders, Dutch, and Norwegians as opposed to the distance segment which is dominated by Italians, Portuguese and Spanish.

The sixth criterion is *Actionability*. Segments should be devised as such so the company can profitably and effectively formulate a marketing mix which will satisfy the needs of the target segment. Basically, the segment should be attractive for the firm and the requirements to address the segment's needs should match the resources and capabilities of the firm. In a cross border setting, actionability becomes a key criteria as not many companies are able to serve at this transnational level. It requires additional resources as well as managerial vision.

Firms need to identify segments for their own market needs. A mobile service company (AxisMobile 2007) came up with three distinct segments taking into account their mobility profiles along with some other demographic and lifestyle features: "Professional super parents" who are professional and busy in constant need of mobile internet while moving around mostly locally for business.

"SOHO" is the second group who does not have much to invest in infrastructure and need to travel for their, often small, businesses such as accountants and consultants; the third group is named "Golden age" referring to tech-aware grandparents who spend several months away from home on travelling or staying in holiday homes. These segments seem viable and attractive to offer mobile email services offered by this firm.

Some transnational mobile segments would meet the above criteria. *Cosmopolitans*, for instance, are immigrants and their descendants characterised by multicultural backgrounds and large families living in multi-ethnic neighbourhoods in urban US (Claritas 2008). Cosmopolitan consumer is "a world citizen—a consumer whose orientation transcends any particular culture or setting" and they are "unfettered by the biases of their home culture" (Cannon and Yaprak 2002, p. 30). When immigrants or mobile populations became part of a segment, mobility or movement becomes an important variable. The difficulty here is the fact that mobile people (migrants and commuters alike) are likely to have multiple reference points guiding their behaviour. This is one reason why international companies are recommended to direct their efforts at customer characteristics rather than country characteristics where degree of cosmopolitan orientation among customers is identified as a powerful segmentation base, reflecting what drives consumers' tastes and preferences (Riefler et al. 2011). These are typical transnational consumers who are open-minded, appreciate diversity, and with consumption patterns transcending borders. Among whom, there can be some *transnational "techno road warriors"* (Schiffman et al. 2008).

References

Aksoy, A. (2006). Transnational virtues and cool loyalties: Responses of Turkish-speaking migrants in London to September 11. *Journal of Ethnic and Migration Studies, 32*(6), 923–946.

Andreasen, A. R. (1966). Geographic mobility and market segmentation. *Journal of Marketing Research, 3*(4), 341–348.

Ariss, A. A., & Syed, J. (2011). Capital mobilization of skilled migrants: A relational perspective. *British Journal of Management, 22*(2), 286–304.

Askegaard, S., Arnould, E. J., & Kjeldgaard, D. (2005). Post-assimilationist ethnic consumer research: Qualifications and extensions. *Journal of Consumer Research, 32*(1), 160–170.

ATEC (Australian Tourism Export Council). (2012). The importance of the working holiday Visa (Subclass 417). *ATEC Position Paper*. Retrieved Feb 10, 2013 from https://www.atec.net.au/0595_whv_positionpaper_lowres_23feb12.pdf.

AxisMobile. (2007). *AxisMobile consumer mobile email marketing segmentation white paper*. Retrieved May 5, 2008, from http://www.axismobile.com/files/AxisMobile_Consumer_Mobile_Email_Marketing_Segmentation_White_Paper.pdf.

Beaverstock, J. V., & Faulconbridge, J. (2010). 'Official' and 'Unofficial' measurements of international business travel to and from the United Kingdom: trends, patterns and limitations. In Beaverstock et al. (Eds.), *International business travel in the global economy* (pp. 57–84). Farnham: Ashgate.

Bell, J. E. (1969). Mobiles—A neglected market segment. *Journal of Marketing, 33*(2), 37–44.

References

Burton, D. (2005). Marketing theory matters. *British Journal of Management, 16*(1), 5–18.

Cannon, H. M., & Yaprak, A. (2002). Will the real-world citizen please stand up! The many faces of cosmopolitan consumer behavior. *Journal of International Marketing, 10*(4), 30–52.

Claritas. (2008). 66 Prizm marketing segments. Claritas Prizm NE. Retrieved June 3, 2008, from http://www.claritas.com/claritas/Default.jsp?ci=3&si=4&pn=prizmne_segments.

Cohen, J. H., Rios, B., & Byars, L. (2009). The value, costs, and meaning of transnational migration in rural Oaxaca, Mexico. *Migration Letters, 6*(1), 15–25.

Cornelius, W. A. & Marcelli, E. A. (2000). *The changing profile of Mexican migrants to the United States: New evidence from California and Mexico. IZA Discussion Papers*, No. 220. http://ftp.iza.org/dp220.pdf.

Craig, C. S., & Douglas, S. P. (2006). Beyond national culture: Implications of cultural dynamics for consumer research. *International Marketing Review, 23*(3), 322–342.

Day, G. S., & Montgomery, D. B. (1999). Charting new directions for marketing. *Journal of Marketing, 63*(special issue), 3–13.

Dickson, P. R. (1981). *An interactionist study of buyer behavior*. PhD dissertation: University of Florida.

Donthu, N., & Cherian, J. (1994). Impact of strength of ethnic identification on Hispanic shopping behavior. *Journal of Retailing, 70*, 383–393.

Dubois, B., Czellar, S., & Laurent, G. (2005). Consumer segments based on attitudes toward luxury: Empirical evidence from twenty countries. *Marketing Letters, 16*(2), 115–128.

Faist, T., Fauser, M., & Reisenauer, E. (2013). *Transnational migration*. Cambridge: Polity Press.

Faulconbridge, J. R., & Beaverstock, J. V. (2008). Geographies of international business travel in the professional service economy. In D. Hislop & D. Hislop (Eds.), *Mobile work/technology: Changing patterns of spatial mobility and mobile technology use in work* (pp. 87–102). London, UK: Routledge.

Figueiredo, B., & Cayla, J. (2012). *The transnational mobility of global cosmopolitans: How multi-acculturation affects the national identities of circulating consumers*. Paper presented at European Marketing Academy Conference (EMAC), Lisbon, Portugal.

Ger, G., & Belk, R. W. (1996). I'd like to buy the world a coke: Consumptionscapes of the "less affluent world". *Journal of Consumer Policy, 19*(3), 271–304.

Gibney, M. J. (2008). Asylum and the expansion of deportation in the United Kingdom. *Government and Opposition, 43*(2), 146–167.

Goldacre, M. J., Davidson, J. M., & Lambert, T. W. (2004). Country of training and ethnic origin of UK doctors: database and survey studies. *British Medical Journal, 329*(7466), 597–600.

Greengrove, K. (2002). Needs-based segmentation: Principles and practice. *International Journal of Market Research, 44*(4), 405–422.

Gustafson, P. (2001). Retirement migration and transnational lifestyles. *Ageing and Society, 21*(4), 371–394.

Harvey, C., & Maclean, M. (2010). Transnational boards and governance regimes: A Franco-British comparison. In M. L. Djelic & S. Quack (Eds.), *Transnational communities* (pp. 107–129). Cambridge: Cambridge University Press.

Haugen, H. Ø., & Carling, J. (2005). On the edge of the Chinese diaspora: The surge of Baihuo business in an African city. *Ethnic and Racial Studies, 28*(4), 639–662.

HESA (Higher Education Statistics Agency). (2012). 2010/11 student and qualifier statistics. http://www.hesa.ac.uk.

Hess, S. (2006). The demand for seasonal farm labor from central- and eastern European Countries in German agriculture. *Agricultural Engineering International: The CIGR Ejournal*. Manuscript MES 05 003. Vol. VIII.

Hill, L., & O'Sullivan, T. (2004). *Foundation marketing*. London: Pearson, Prentice Hall.

Hurun. (2012). *The Chinese luxury traveler white paper 2012*. Shanghai: Hurun Research Institute. http://img.hurun.net/hmec/2012-06-04/201206040930327901.pdf.

Illes, S. (2005). Elderly immigration to Hungary. *Migration Letters, 2*(2), 164–169.

IPA (Institute of Practitioners in Advertising). (2012). Retrieved Jan 13, 2013, from www.ipa.co.uk/News/IPA-publishes-report-on-Britains-ethnic-minorities.

ITU (International Telecommunications Union). (2007). *ITU World communication/ICT indicators database*. Retrieved Jan 3, 2009 from http://www.itu.int/ITU-D/ict/statistics/.

Itzigsohn, J., Cabral, C. D., Medina, E. H., & Vazquez, O. (1999). Mapping Dominican transnationalism: Narrow and broad transnational practices. *Ethnic and Racial Studies, 22*(2), 316–339.

Khattab, N., Johnston, R., Sirkeci, I., & Modood, T. (2010). The impact of spatial segregation on the employment outcomes amongst Bangladeshi men and women in England and Wales. *Sociological Research Online, 15*(1), 3.

Kotler, P., & Keller, K. L. (2008). *Marketing management* (13th ed.). London, UK: Pearson, Prentice Hall.

Lee, W., & Tse, D. K. (1994). Changing media consumption in a new home: Acculturation patterns among Hong Kong immigrants to Canada. *Journal of Advertising, 23*, 57–70.

Lin, X., & Tao, S. (2012). Transnational entrepreneurs: Characteristics, drivers, and success factors. *Journal of International Entrepreneurship, 10*(1), 50–69.

Martin, P. L. (2013). Migration and US agricultural competitiveness. *Migration Letters, 10*(2), 159–179.

Mendenhall, M., & Oddou, G. (1985). The dimensions of expatriate acculturation: A review. *The Academy of Management Review, 10*(1), 39–47.

Millar, J., & Salt, J. (2008). *International students and the labour market: experience in the UK*. Paper presented at Leverhulme Programme Conference on Mobility in International Labour Markets, University College London, UK.

MOHnz (Ministry of Health New Zealand). (2008). Doctors in New Zealand. Retrieved June 10, 2008, from http://www.moh.govt.nz/moh.nsf/wpg_Index/About-Statistics+about+doctors.

Morawska, E. (2004). Immigrant transnational entrepreneurs in New York: Three varieties and their correlates. *International Journal of Entrepreneurial Behaviour & Research, 10*(5), 325–348.

NICE & GDP. (2012). *Dreams and schemes in Queens New York, immigrant struggles to find work and get status in the face of consumer fraud*. Report by New York Immigrant Community Empowerment and the Community Development Project. Retrieved Feb 10, 2013 from http://www.cdp-ny.org/report/DreamsandSchemes.pdf.

Ofcom. (2003). *Reaching the ethnic consumer: A challenge for marketers*. Ofcom Report. Retrieved Feb 2, 2013, from http://www.ofcom.org.uk/static/archive/bsc/pdfs/research/ethnic.pdf.

O'Leary, A. O. (2009). The ABCs of migration costs: Assembling, bajadores, and coyotes. *Migration Letters, 6*(1), 27–36.

ONS (Office for National Statistics). (2006). *Travel trends*. Retrieved May 5, 2008, from http://www.statistics.gov.uk.

ONS (Office for National Statistics). (2012a). *Internal migration by local authorities in England and Wales, year ending June 2011*. Statistical Bulletin, Retrieved September 25, 2012, from http://www.ons.gov.uk/ons/dcp171778_280054.pdf.

ONS (Office for National Statistics). (2012b, September). *Overseas travel and tourism—monthly release*. Retrieved November 15, 2012, from http://www.ons.gov.uk/ons/rel/ott/overseas-travel-and-tourism—monthly-release/september-2012/index.html.

Özden, C., & Schiff, M. (Eds.). (2005). *International migration, remittances and the brain drain*. Washington: World Bank and Palgrave Macmillan.

Portes, A., & Shafer, S. (2006). *Revisiting the enclave hypothesis: Miami twenty-five years later*. CMD Working Paper No.06-10, Princeton University. Retrieved Feb 2, 2013 from http://www.princeton.edu/cmd/working-papers/papers/wp0610.pdf.

Portes, A., Guarnizo, L. E., & Haller, W. J. (2002). Transnational entrepreneurs: An alternative form of immigrant economic adaptation. *American Sociological Review, 67*(2), 278–298.

Quigley, J. M., & Weinberg, D. H. (1977). Intra-urban residential mobility: a review and synthesis. *International Regional Science Review, 2*(1), 41–66.

References

Riefler, P., Diamantopoulos, A., & Siguaw, J. A. (2011). Cosmopolitan consumers as a target group for segmentation. *Journal of International Business Studies, 43*(3), 285–305.

Salt, J., & Wood, P. (2013). Acquisition and mobility of expertise in global corporate labour markets. In T. Modood & J. Salt (Eds.), *Global migration, ethnicity and britishness* (pp. 84–107). Palgrave: Basingstoke.

Saxenian, A. L. (2002). From brain drain to brain circulation: Transnational communities and regional upgrading in India and China. *Studies in Comparative International Development, 40*(2), 35–61.

Saxenian, A. L. (2006). *The new argonauts: Regional advantage in a global economy.* Cambridge: Harvard University Press.

Schiffman, L., Kanuk, L., & Hansen, H. (2008). *Consumer behaviour: A European outlook.* London: Pearson, Prentice Hall.

Sirkeci, I. (2009). Ethnic marketing potential in England and Wales: New evidence from the 2001 UK census. *Asian Journal of Marketing, 2*(1), 1–9.

Sirkeci, I., Mannix, R., & Bologna, L. (2010). *Who cares about research? Role of research reputation in business school marketing in England.* Paper presented at the Academy of Marketing Annual Conference, Coventry University, July 6–8, 2010, Coventry, UK.

Smetherham, C., Fenton, S., & Modood, T. (2008). *How global is higher education in the UK?* Paper presented at Leverhulme Programme Conference on Mobility in International Labour Markets, University College London, UK.

Smith, W. R. (1956). Product differentiation and market segmentation as alternative marketing strategies. *The Journal of Marketing, 21*(1), 3–8.

Sudbury, L., & Simcock, P. (2009). A multivariate segmentation model of senior consumers. *Journal of Consumer Marketing, 26*(4), 251–262.

Tan, Y., Richardson, S., Lester, L., Bai, T., & Sun, M. L. (2009). Evaluation of Australia's Working Holiday Maker (WHM) program. Department of immigration and citizenship. Retrieved Feb 10, 2013 from http://www.immi.gov.au/media/publications/research/_pdf/whm-report.pdf.

Terjesen, S., & Elam, A. (2009). Transnational entrepreneurs' venture internationalization strategies: A practice theory approach. *Entrepreneurship: Theory and Practice, 33*(5), 1093–1120.

UKBA (UK Border Agency). (2007). Previous earnings. Retrieved June 6, 2012, from http://www.ukba.homeoffice.gov.uk/sitecontent/documents/policyandlaw/ecis/hsmpcaseworkerguidance/previousearnings.pdf?view=Binary.

UNDP (Population Division of the Department of Economic and Social Affairs of the United Nations Secretariat). (2008). *Trends in total migrant stock: The 2005 revision.* Retrieved May 5, 2008, from http://esa.un.org/migration.

USDoC (US Department of Commerce, Office of Travel and Tourism Industries from the Bureau of Economic Analysis). (2012, June). *Latest statistics.* from http://tinet.ita.doc.gov/.

Üstüner, T., & Holt, D. B. (2007). Dominated consumer acculturation: The social construction of poor migrant women's consumer identity projects in a Turkish squatter. *Journal of Consumer Research, 34*(1), 41–56.

Venkatesh, A. (1995). Ethnoconsumerism: A new paradigm to study cultural and cross-cultural consumer behavior. In J. A. Costa & G. J. Bamossy (Eds.), *Marketing in a multicultural world, ethnicity, nationalism, and cultural identity* (pp. 26–27). Thousand Oaks: Sage Publication.

Wang, L. (2004). An Investigation of Chinese Immigrant Consumer Behaviour inToronto, Canada. *Journal of Retailing and Consumer Services, 11,* 307–320.

Webster, C. (1994). Effects of Hispanic ethnic identification on marital roles in the purchase decision process. *Journal of Consumer Research, 21,* 319–331.

Wedel, M., & Kamakura, W. A. (2000). *Market segmentation, conceptual and methodological foundations, 2nd Edition.* ISQM8. Boston: Kluwer Academic Publishers.

Weinstein, A. (2004). *Handbook of market segmentation: Strategic targeting for business and technology firms.* London: Routledge.

Wind, Y. (1978). Issues and advances in segmentation research. *Journal of Marketing Research, 15*(3), 317–337.

Zhou, M. (2004). Revisiting ethnic entrepreneurship: convergencies, controversies, and conceptual advancements. *International Migration Review, 38*(3), 1040–1074.

Chapter 4
Targeting and Reaching Transnationals and Transnational Mobiles

So far we have established that a significantly large mobile population is out there; immigrants, tourists, students and connected others. The total numbers are expressed in hundreds of millions. Then we also have a potentially larger number of consumers we call transnationals, including cosmopolitans. The challenge in terms of targeting is apparent. Once the transnational and mobile segments are identified, marketing managers need to select only customers that their organisation can serve well and profitably. This can be done by employing multiple segmentation bases while integrating mobility and movement in their sets of variables. Segmenting customers with similar characteristics across national boundaries is common for many companies such as BMW or Mercedes with their high end cars targeting an affluent group of customers across the world. Some of these customers are non-mobile transnationals while others are mobiles, including immigrants and minority clients.

It is not only about how to reach these customers but also sometimes the risks associated with such effort. For example, immigrant minorities and cultural differences has been a delicate issue in many countries. Hence, many organisations might have just avoided special marketing programmes targeting those transnational consumers since they were concerned about backlash. Despite sizeable segments known in the UK, only very few major firms in banking and mobile services have made inroads to target, for example, Polish, Asian and other minority customers. Nevertheless, within ethnic enclaves, there is strong evidence of targeting many immigrant and minority groups using ethnic languages, ethnic media, and offering ethnic oriented marketing mixes.

I. Sirkeci, *Transnational Marketing and Transnational Consumers*,
SpringerBriefs in Business, DOI: 10.1007/978-3-642-36775-5_4,
© The Author(s) 2013

Box 2. Transnational satellite TV channels

Transnational TV channels target linguistic, ethnic, and religious communities across national boundaries. For example, Turkish-speaking consumers in Turkey, Europe and other places can tune into various channels broadcasting in Turkish and Kurdish. These include Turkish state broadcasting TRT, and many national stations including ATV, CNN Turk, Kanal D, NTV, Show TV, Star, Sky Turk as well as others, for instance, Roj TV, Kurdsat, Yol TV, imece TV targeting minority groups including Kurds and Alevis. Furthermore, there are specific channels originating from provinces and towns in Turkey. These can target specific small sub-segments as well as larger transnational groups for example the Kurds in Europe, Turkey, Iraq, Iran, Syria and elsewhere. Availability of these channels is crucial for the acculturation process of these transnational segments. A viewer from London says; "That's why we change channels, move across different channels, to have more knowledge, to be reassured, to be better informed" (Aksoy 2006, p. 937).

Today, there are certain established channels available nationwide as well as locally to reach these transnational consumers. Internet offers a very rich portfolio to reach specific groups despite some shortcomings such as the difficulty in identifying individuals at IP level in households. At the same time, there are transnational satellite channels now well established. Organisations targeting transnationals are already using these outlets. Aksoy (2006, p. 926) points to a shift from "national broadcasting systems" to "the advent of transnational channels such as Zee TV, Asianet, Sony Asia, MBC, Al-Jazeera, Phoenix or the Chinese Channel since the 1990s". Available TV channels to Turkish and Kurdish consumers are presented in Box 2. From a marketing point of view, there are two advantages: (a) Viewers can watch these channels wherever they go, (b) organisations communicating to them can use these channels. For broadcasters, this is protecting consumer loyalty to an extent against the available channels in the destination country. For consumers, it may reduce the costs of movement, they may not feel the need to find new channels to watch. Hence it helps to restrict switching behaviour. Nevertheless, this availability is also facilitating wider comparison as noted in Box 1 about TV channels.

Despite these advances in ethnic media, there is still difficulty in reaching these customers through the mainstream media which is rarely followed by these transnationals (e.g. Gray 2007, p. 31). Hence alternative channels are the way forward. Spatial concentration of transnationals and mobiles (including minorities) offers some help. Marketers can target these particular areas and routes to reach them by the help of geo-demographic analysis distinguishing mobiles and non-mobiles and sub-segments within.

The ubiquitous availability of internet and wireless connections, as well as smart devices, can be useful for marketers in tackling this challenge as they enable

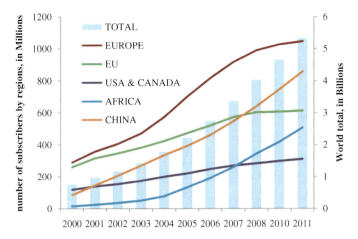

Fig. 4.1 Mobile phone subscribers by world regions, 2000–2011. *Source* ITU (http://www.itu.int/ITU-D/ict/statistics/)

more personalised targeting. Smart devices and mobile internet is also useful for targeting people on the move. Better regulated roaming charges across borders means reduced barriers and interruption to such services available to transnationally mobile consumers. It is possible that additional charges are likely to interrupt the connection between the offer and the consumer and, in return, the transaction potential is lost. The evidence shows that there is good potential to develop further customised communication to target transnationals and mobiles as over the recent years, advertising on mobile devices has gained increasing market share. Advances in digital technologies and online services are at marketers disposal to target even very small groups through "narrowcasting" (Waterman 1992; Smith-Shomade 2002), "niche marketing" (Anderson 2006), "micro-marketing" (Armstrong and Kotler 2007) and "mass customisation" (Coletti and Aichner 2011; Bardakci and Whitelock 2003).

Mass customisation, individual and local marketing are all referring to micromarketing where small groups or individual customers are served. Custom-made suits by a tailor or furniture to order cabinets are examples of such individual marketing or *markets-of-one marketing*. Nike ID (nikeid.nike.com) is considered to be a pioneer successful case for mass customisation. It allows customers to personalise and design the products to their own liking online, in store or via post. Adidas, Reebok, and Converse are all offer similar services. It seems despite the challenges such as customisation requires intensive customer involvement, delays in the delivery of the product, more expensive than standard products, Nike ID proved to be successful. Mark Parker, the CEO of Nike, nearly four years ago, said that they are more worried about what customers are up to than about their rivals and he led the drive towards letting his customers design their own ways to personalize Nike products for their lifestyles. He was the force behind NIKEiD which allowed customers to customize anything that they want to put on their feet, heads or bodies (Horovitz 2009).

In Fig. 4.1, the growth of mobile phone subscriptions in the world since 2000 is outlined: While overall volume grew from 738 million to over 5 billion, Africa and China registered the fastest growth. As elaborated in an earlier study, mobile services facilitating connectivity are crucial for reaching mobile customers (see Sirkeci and Mannix 2010). Consumers and business people are connected in today's world of ubiquitous, pervasive, invisible and mobile computing nodes (Valavanis et al. 2003, p. 2). Interactive, personalised and constant connectivity paves the way for new marketing opportunities with the help of location based services (Bauer et al. 2005; Barnes 2003). The fact that mobile phone users usually have their devices with them at all times allows the advertisers to contact individual customers anytime and anywhere (Bauer et al. 2005, p. 182). Typically, the SIM (Subscriber Identity Module) cards are owned and registered by individuals and therefore exact identification of each user is possible. The downside is that many customers despise mass advertising and reject the messages (Godin 2001 cited in Sirkeci and Mannix 2010). Therefore, only rather carefully crafted marketing communication perceived as valuable by customers will do the trick. Internet and mobile service usage patterns also need to be combined with mobility patterns. For example, growth of social media and virtual communities prompted a rapid growth of review sites, blogs and forums users of which are likely to be more critical of product and service offerings.

References

Aksoy, A. (2006). Transnational virtues and cool loyalties: Responses of Turkish-speaking migrants in London to september 11. *Journal of Ethnic and Migration Studies, 32*(6), 923–946.

Gray, R, (2007). Immigration, world of opportunity. *The Marketer*, November, 28–31.

Waterman, D. (1992). "Narrowcasting" and "Broadcasting" on nonbroadcast media, a program choice model. *Communication Research, 19*(1), 3–28.

Smith-Shomade, B. E. (2002). Narrowcasting in the new world information order, a space for the audience? *Television & New Media, 5*(1), 69–81.

Anderson, C. (2006). *The long tail: Why the future of business is selling less of more.* New York: Hyperion.

Armstrong, G., & Kotler, P. (2007). *Marketing: An introduction* (8th ed.). New Jersey: Pearson Prentice Hall.

Coletti, P., & Aichner, T. (2011). *Mass customization: An exploration of European characteristics.* Heidelberg: Springer.

Bardakci, A., & Whitelock, J. (2003). Mass-customization in marketing: The consumer perspective. *Journal of Consumer Marketing, 20*(5), 463–479.

Horovitz, B. (2009). CEO Mark Parker works on keeping Nike cool. *USA Today.* Retrieved August, 2009, from http://usatoday30.usatoday.com/money/industries/retail/2009-12-07-nike07_CV_N.htm.

References

Sirkeci, I., & Mannix, R. (2010). Segmentation challenges posed by 'transnationals' in mobile marketing. In Key Pousttchi & D. G. Wiedemann (Eds.), *The handbook of research on mobile marketing management* (pp. 94–114). New York: IGI Global.

Valavanis, E., Ververidis, C., Vazirgianis, M. & Polyzos, G.C. (2003) MobiShare: Sharing context-dependent data and services among mobile devices. Retrieved Jan 3, 2009, from http://www.db-net.aueb.gr.

Bauer, H. H., Barnes, S. J., Reichardt, T., & Neumann, M. M. (2005). Driving consumer acceptance of mobile marketing: A theoretical framework and empirical study. *Journal of Electronic Commerce Research, 6*(3), 181–192.

Barnes, S. J. (2003). Location-based services: The state of the art. *E-Service Journal, 2*(3), 59–70.

Chapter 5
Conclusions

We have discussed the transnationality of the organisation in reference to the UNCTAD's measurement. Although it makes sense to analyse the spread of assets, employees, and sales of a firm across national borders, it is also important to consider the role of transnational business mentality when setting up marketing strategies. It determines the transnationality of marketing and of the organisation. What matters is the *transnationality*, the degree of connectedness between consumers across national boundaries; and the degree of connectedness and exchanges within and between organisations across national borders and boundaries. Mobility and movement are key to this but connectedness is also achieved without movement of individuals or groups of customers. While increasing transnational connectedness and mobility moderating consumers needs, wants and desires, firms and organisations need to adjust their marketing strategies accordingly.

Transnationally mobile consumers often face changes in the marketing environment as they move around. These include changes in terms of political, legal, socio-cultural, and technological environment but also changes in the *consumptionscape*. Some products and services may not be available or may be offered and consumed differently in different destinations. For example, one noticeable implication for brands and marketers here is consumer loyalty and switching behaviour. Customers may switch more often as some brands may not be available in their new place of residence. While some brands benefit from it, that is in acquiring new customers and potential access to new markets, others will suffer as they will lose loyal customers.

Transnational connectedness and mobility also likely to have an effect on marketing mix formulations. For instance, when it is possible to check prices of certain products and services across the world over the internet, it will not be easy to justify different prices in different countries. This is more so for regions such as the European Union where cross border trade is virtually free and shipping costs are relatively low. Hence for a British or Dutch consumer buying online from Germany can be as hassle free as buying online from local online stores such as Amazon. For internet savvy consumers, worldwide comparisons are more likely.

I. Sirkeci, *Transnational Marketing and Transnational Consumers*,
SpringerBriefs in Business, DOI: 10.1007/978-3-642-36775-5_5,
© The Author(s) 2013

The growing importance of transnational firms, transnational consumers, and as a result, of transnational marketing dictates some emerging needs such as transnational regulations too. For example, the EU and similar regional unions are already implementing regulations for cross-border consumer transactions, that is to say consumers purchasing goods and services from other countries (Twigg-Flesner 2012, pp. 2–3). Yet, it is equally important to consider regulations regarding transactions of those *consumers who are transnationally mobile* within the EU and elsewhere. The Rome-I Regulation, article 6, suggests that consumer disputes are subject to the law of the country where they have their habitual residence. The question, then, becomes what if the habitual residence is in more than one place, more than one country? The challenge here is to abandon the paradigm of "habitual residence in one country" in favour of a more fluid and dynamic concept of residence(s) to cover not only cross-border transactions but also the transactions of those crossing borders. This means more harmonisation is required to avoid potential conflicts arising from different legislations across national borders.

In an increasingly transnational world, organisations tend to invest in long-term cross-border relationships with national, local governments as well as with the public. For example, Jeffrey Garten, a former administration official said that, "Companies that establish deep local roots and show, by dint of example rather than empty rhetoric, that their strategies are aligned with the long-term goals of the host country stand the best chance of persevering." (Kimmitt et al. 2010, p. 65). This has to be part of transnational mentality in borderless business strategy. At the same time, transnational firms and organisations need to adjust their business strategies where mobility of staff is seen as a value added rather than a cost element. Integrated mobility strategy may enhance cross cultural leadership skills pool and enable movement of capability between different markets where the firm operates. This is another area of investigation which may benefit many organisations.

It is called a *Global Village* not because everybody is identical in that village but because everybody is very mobile and on the move at all times while also being connected ubiquitously. Improved telecommunications and greater economic and political integration are among the factors making such high mobility and connectedness possible. Despite some convergence and emergence of some degree of common understanding, there are still many distinctive national and local consumer characteristics that influence marketing decisions at national and local levels. Nevertheless, the transnationals, transnational mobile consumers display some common characteristics in terms of mobility and connectedness. High level of diversity among the transnationals (i.e. many sub-segments) are likely to limit the potential for building economies of scale. As mentioned earlier, micromarketing, including individual marketing and mass customisation may offer the right instruments to address distinct needs of smaller sub-segments with more customized products and services. There is already evidence showing the success of such marketing effort (e.g. NikeID).

This does not mean internationally mobile groups are an easy to identify and reach market segment. Some sectors are more likely to advance such as telecommunication and transportation while others will follow from a distance. Likewise some countries have rather mixed populations with more transnational links. Organisations in such countries may take the lead. In the UK, for example, some companies moved ahead when they targeted the Polish transnationals or Muslim customers (Sirkeci and Mannix 2010).

Marketers and researchers need to focus on the ways in which we can understand, identify and profile transnational mobile customers and their varying needs and wants. Then marketers will be matching these to the availability of services, firms and capacities to serve such customers linked across borders and constantly mobile. Organisations with transnational orientation and with culturally diverse, or transnational, teams are likely to understand and address the transnational segments' needs and wants rather easily.

Future research on transnational consumer behaviour should focus on measurable markers of mobile consumers and connected consumers. In earlier studies and here, movement, mobility patterns, commuting distance, and change of place of residence are suggested as useful segmentation variables to capture transnational mobile consumers. Connectedness is also possible to be identified through these variables and household compositions. Then the influence of multiple cultural reference points needs to be measured. Country of origin for products, services and brands has been studied pretty extensively. Now same can be done for the customers. It may lead us to revisit exiting segmentation models and methods.

In business to business markets, this can be assessed by firm networks and diversity of staff profiles. In the first half of the book, the UNCTAD's definition of transnational companies is examined and the accuracy is questioned. The methodology is a simple mean calculation of the percentage of assets, employees, and sales abroad for the firm in question. The proposal here is to add a fourth dimension. The transnational orientation in marketing strategy is likely to make an impact on firms' success.

References

Twigg-Flesner, C. (2012). *A cross-border only regulation for consumer transactions in the EU*. New York: Springer.

Kimmitt, R., Garay, M., & Allen, D. (2010). Money and borders: Cross-border investments in a changing global market place. *Deloitte Review, 6*, 56–69.

Sirkeci, I., & Mannix, R. (2010). Segmentation challenges posed by 'transnationals' in mobile marketing. In Key Pousttchi & Dietmar G. Wiedemann (Eds.), *The handbook of research on mobile marketing management* (pp. 94–114). New York: IGI Global.

About the Author

Ibrahim Sirkeci is Professor of Transnational Studies and Marketing and Director of Regent's Centre for Transnational Studies (RCTS) at Regent's University London. He is leading the MA in International Marketing at European Business School London. He holds a Ph.D. from the University of Sheffield (UK) and a B.A. in Political Science and Public Administration from Bilkent University (Turkey). His main areas of expertise are human mobility, conflict, transnational marketing and consumers, marketing of business schools, labour markets, remittances, segmentation and digital piracy. Previously, he worked at the University of Bristol and Hacettepe University, Bilkent University and a private university in Turkey. Prof. Sirkeci has taught International Marketing, Transnational Marketing, Consumer Behaviour, and Principles of Marketing to diverse student groups at universities in the UK, Germany and Turkey. He has been consulted by the World Bank, European Parliament, Turkish Government and Euromonitor. Prof. Sirkeci has published several books and reports, many articles and frequently contributed to conferences in Europe and the US. Prof. Sirkeci is also serving on editorial boards of several scholarly journals while at the same time editing *Transnational Marketing Journal* and *Migration Letters* journal. His most recent books include *Migration and Remittances during the Global Financial Crisis and Beyond* published by the World Bank (2012) and *Cultures of Migration* published by the University of Texas Press (2011) and selected as *Outstanding Academic Title* by the *Choice* magazine in the US. He can be reached at sirkeci1@regents.ac.uk.

I. Sirkeci, *Transnational Marketing and Transnational Consumers*,
SpringerBriefs in Business, DOI: 10.1007/978-3-642-36775-5,
© The Author(s) 2013

Index

B
Bartlett, 7, 13–15, 18
BAT, 20
Beamish, 7
Bebo, 27
BMW, 59

C
Cayla, 35
Circulating consumers, 35
Commonwealth of Independent
   States (CIS), 53
Connectedness, 11, 25–27, 29, 66
Consumptionscape, 65
Cosmopolitan, 53, 54
Cross-border networks, 28
Cultural reference points, 26, 32

D
Danone, 20

E
e-geography, 28
Elseve, 18
Ethnocentric, 15
Ethnocentric-Polycentric-Regiocentric-
   Geocentric (EPRG), 14

F
Facebook, 27, 44
Faist, 44, 49
Frost and Sullivan, 20

G
Geocentric, 15
Global consumers, 25
Globalisation, 4
Global Marketing, 14
Glocal, 2, 4
Green, 11
Gross Domestic Product
   (GDP), 6

H
H&M, ix, 20
Harzing, 6
Hollensen, viii, 5, 14

I
Imagined community
   of consumers, 29
Integrating agents, 5
*International baby food action
   network*, 17
International marketing, 13
Intra-company transfers, 41

K
Keegan, 11

L
Levitt, 4, 15
LinkedIn, 27
L'Oreal, 18
LVMH, 20

Index

M
Marketing mix, 13, 15
Marriott, 50
Mass customisation, 61
Micromarketing, 61, 66
Mobile consumers. *See* Transnational mobile
    consumers
Mobility, vii, 1–4, 11, 12, 25, 26, 29, 35, 37,
    54, 66
Moët Hennessy Louis Vuitton (LVMH), 20
Movement, vii, 2, 4, 26, 29, 35, 38, 54
Multinational marketing, 13
MySpace, 27

N
National allegiance, 35
Nestle, 17, 19
Nike, 61

O
Oriflame, 19

R
Reebok, 61
Regent's, 46, 69

S
Sojourners, 48
Steven Vertovec, 2
Stonehouse, 11

T
The EU, 66
The globals, 4

Total global strategy, 18
Transnational communities, 3
Transnational companies (TNCs), ix, 6
Transnational cosmopolitanism, 26
Transnational imagined communities, 29
Transnationality, 3
Transnationality index, 4
Transnationality spread index, 5
Transnationally mobile capital, 5
Transnationally oriented, 26
Transnational management, 13
Transnational mentality, 11, 15
Transnational mobile consumers, vii, 3, 66
Transnational mobiles, 25
Transnational orientation, 15
Transnationals, 4, 35, 36, 66
Turkey, 1, 32, 37, 42, 44, 49, 69

U
Unilever, 19
United Nations Conference on Trade and
    Development (UNCTAD), ix, 5, 7, 11,
    12, 17, 19, 65, 67

V
Vertovec, 3
Virtual geography, 28

W
Wasilevski, 19

Printed by Publishers' Graphics LLC
MLSI130522.15.15.78